10699031

INTIMACY WITH GOD

Intimacy with God

DONALD G. MOSTROM

Guideposts

CARMEL • NEW YORK 10512

Intimacy With God was originally published as
The Dynamics of Intimacy With God.

This Guideposts edition is published by
special arrangement with Tyndale House Publishers.

The quotation taken from *Instruction in Faith* by
John Calvin, translated and edited by Paul T.
Fuhrmann, copyright © MCMXLIX, by W. L.
Jenkins, is used by permission of The Westminster
Press.

Scripture quotations from the *New American
Standard Bible,* copyright © The Lockman
Foundation 1960, 1962, 1963, 1968, 1971, 1972,
1973, 1975, 1977, are used by permission.

Scripture quotations taken from the *New English
Bible* copyright © 1976 by Oxford University Press
are used by permission.

Scripture quotations taken from *The Holy Bible,
New International Version,* copyright © 1978 by the
New York International Bible Society are used by
permission.

Scripture quotations taken from the *Revised
Standard Version of the Bible,* copyright © 1942,
1952, 1971, 1973 are used by permission.

First Printing, October 1983
Library of Congress Catalog Card Number 83-50317
ISBN 0-8423-0615-3
Copyright © 1983 by Donald G. Mostrom
All rights reserved
Printed in the United States of America

To Robert and Mildred McCullough

Many in Christ's family, including this author,
rise up and call them blessed.

CONTENTS

PREFACE

In physics the word *dynamics* refers to the application of force to an object, with resulting motion. These days the word is used in many nontechnical ways. We speak of the *dynamics* of any operation and mean the principles or powers that make it work. Richard Lovelace gives the term a Christian application in the title of his book, *Dynamics of Spiritual Life*. He refers to the way in which the power of God becomes effective in Christian experience.

This is a matter of much concern to Christians. The gospel is a message of hope and carries with it the expectation of power to transform everyday life. But expectation and realization are often far apart, so much so that many believers in Christ become skeptical about the practical possibilities of their faith. This is a much too frequent tragedy—and tragedy it is! Anything that diminishes our realistic grasp of the wonder of Christ's redeeming work should be viewed with sorrow.

What Dr. Lovelace has done as a historical theologian, I now seek to express as biblical theology. This is essentially a study of Scripture teaching—an attempt to lay out briefly but comprehensively the doctrines of life with God. It considers both negative and positive dynamics: that is, what the Bible teaches about forces that make it difficult for us to experience the transforming power of God in our lives, and the way in which He designed to make His power work in our experience.

What underlies this task and justifies it is the conviction that the Bible is the rule for both faith *and life*. It was not given simply to provide materials for a creed that would be unrelated to Monday-through-Friday at the shop—nor even simply to tell us what ought to be true at the shop without telling us how it can be done. Rather it is totally sufficient to guide us into the experience of God's power. Properly confronted, Scripture will teach us the responses of faith in such a way as to produce the life we long for with increasing effect.

The hope of the author is that this work will be treated as a manual for the prayerful study of Scripture. Small group Bible studies can be a fruitful way to grapple with these truths.

Haste will tend to limit the profit which can be gained from this study. The thoughts of the Word are sometimes profound and its implications many. The Holy Spirit is the great "Anointing that teaches," and will surely respond to you if you seek His mind in the Word of God. This requires time, prayer, and meditation.

The author is deeply grateful to those who have supported him in this project. The steady emphasis on careful and prayerful study of Scripture at the Peniel Bible Conference in Lake Luzerne, New York, has for many years provided a fruitful scene for the development of biblical insights.

Teachers such as the late G. Travers Sloyer, the late Susan E. Beers, and the late Raymond M. Meiners, to name but three, have been stimulating co-searchers of the Word. The author acknowledges with gratitude the help given through careful reading of the manuscript by Julian Alexander, James Brownson, William C. Brownson, Jr., Howard W. Ferrin, James Huber, Ed Huff, and Richard F. Lovelace. In several cases the wives of these men read the manuscript and made profitable suggestions.

The author's wife, Joyce, gave constant encouragement and prayerful support in the same way that she has made all his life blessed.

ONE

The Place of Fellowship

God desires fellowship with human beings.

That's a remarkable thought! Somehow He seems so complete and self-sufficient that it's incredible He would desire anything at all. But God desires an intimate relationship with each of us. We cannot read far in the Bible without becoming aware of this.

God's making us "in his image" (Gen. 1:26, 27) indicates this. The image of God cannot refer to our physical being, since God is spirit and has no bodily form. It must refer to the kind of personality we have: to our mental and emotional characteristics, our powers of choice, our moral attributes—all patterned after God's personality. After creation, it immediately became possible for God to interact with His human creatures. He talked with them. It is apparent that He loved them and wanted their love.

Fellowship is a good word for the kind of relationship that God designed for Himself and His creature. In

Eden it was shown at once to be a *two-way* interaction. It was not God's intention to create beings whose identity and function would be wiped out by His own greatness. He did not plan to create shells or mere puppets to manipulate. He designed whole persons. He called on them to operate at full capacity. He expected them to rule the rest of creation. There was to be fellowship with Himself in all this—indeed submission and obedience—but it was to be a fellowship in which two complete persons were interacting. The One is infinite and the other finite; the One limitless and the other limited. But both are *whole*. Genesis 2 presents to us a delightful picture of God bringing the animals to Adam "to see what he would name them" (Gen. 2:19, NIV). If "naming" involved discovery of the true character and identity of these creatures, this was perhaps a far greater discovery than we might realize, carried out in a marvelous, functioning fellowship with the living God.

This scene of beauty was wrecked by the appearance of evil. But the subsequent record of Scripture indicates that God still desired fellowship with human beings. What extraordinary measures He took to secure it! He set up covenants with mankind which show this desire. He designed a tabernacle, temple, and priestly system with great precision in order that He might live with His people. "Love me with all your heart" became the great commandment from God (Deut. 6:5). It indicated not just the top requirement set by God for our behavior, but also His deep desire to be known and loved by His human creatures and to interact with them.

He steadily spoke to them. Right from the start there was a redemptive note in His speaking. He began at once to reveal that He would work out the reversal of their fall, the destruction of their enemy, and a removal of the curse which had come on them. Until that time, He would provide ways for a chosen people to draw near to Him and count Him their God. His desire for them was never far from the surface. His hurt at their hardness was sometimes deep: "All day long I have held out my hands to an obstinate people" (Isa. 65:2, NIV).

He not only spoke to them again and again, but He entered into a process by which his redemptive speaking was recorded and preserved in written form. And how is this process described? "All Scripture is *God-breathed!*" says Paul (2 Tim. 3:16, NIV). How *intimate!* Scripture is the out-breathing of God's heart. Though it reveals His holiness and stern justice, throughout its pages it is charged with His longing, His loving, His desire to recover a people for Himself.

The fact that we were designed for fellowship with God is crucial. There are many things about God, redemption, ourselves, and our problems that we will not understand until we see them in this light.

1. *We will not understand our human sickness until we see it as the result of our alienation from God.* We are *healthy,* in the deepest and widest sense of that word, only if we are in fellowship with our God. Like an intricate machine designed for a particular use but used for something else, we break down in a variety of ways

when not functioning with God. It is like trying to pound a nail with a bar of soap. Our minds do not function rightly when they are not in fellowship with God and "thinking His thoughts after Him." Our emotions are out of balance unless His love and grace are being shared in that area of life. Our wills are perverted; our appetites hurt us; our relationships suffer.

2. *We will not understand our human problem until we realize that our alienation from God is more than simply passive.* "Dead in trespasses and sins" (Eph. 2:1, NASB) may sound passive, but the fact of the matter is that active rebellion has intruded upon our intimacy with God. We came to love our freedom from God with a passion that we give to few other things. We not only *are* alienated from Him, but we prize that independence, guard it jealously, express it in a thousand subtle ways, and strike out at anything that threatens it—even God!

In this book I am describing this active thrust of our fallen nature as the quality of *independency.* As I am using it, *independency* will have a particular and negative meaning. While "independence" can often have a "good" sense (as, for example, when it is the opposite of an unhealthy kind of dependence), I will consistently use the word *independency* to refer to the human drive for personal sovereignty, the desire to be without accountability to any other person.

3. *We will not understand redemption until we see the goal of it, not simply as the forgiveness of our sins*

and the securing of a final home in heaven, but as "God in Christ reconciling the world to Himself" (2 Cor. 5:19, NASB). God's design, as He abolishes the old covenants, temples, and priestly systems, is to make *us* His temple and fill our lives with His living presence. His longing and our deepest needs are met in the restoration of fellowship. Through Christ's work we may now once more "walk humbly with [our] God" (Micah 6:8, NIV).

4. *We will also have an incomplete understanding of our redemption if we think of it only as a benefit to be enjoyed individually, that is, affecting only our private relationship with God.* Back in the original scene in Genesis another important aspect of fellowship appears. God made human beings in His own image in order that He might interact with those who were like Himself—thought to thought, heart to heart, will to will. But in designing for this He also made provision for human social relationships as well. Indeed, we hear God saying, "It is not good for the man to be alone; I will make a helper suitable for him" (Gen. 2:18, NIV).

It's astounding to think of God saying that something about His creation was not good! It was not that there was anything wrong with what He had made—only that it was not yet complete. In designing the man to have fellowship with Himself, He had also determined that those same characteristics would be expressed with other human beings with a similar nature. Adam was not alone in the God-ward sense; he had God with him. But he also needed a human companion, and until he had one, something was incomplete. Something was "not good."

The word *suitable* in the phrase "suitable for him" is significant. The literal meaning of the Hebrew words is "someone over against him," that is, someone who is comparable to him corresponding to him, *like* him. Lower animals were brought to him, but lacked something essential in their makeup. They were not *like* him. Biologically there were many similarities. They were not, however, made in the image of God in the same sense as he was, so were not comparable, not corresponding to him. They were not suitable because he could not have fellowship with creatures that were not persons in the same way that he was.

So God made woman as He had made man, in His image. This made it possible for her to have fellowship with God, like Adam could. But it also filled that created need for human fellowship. Human social interactions were part of God's great design for fellowship.

The spoiling of fellowship with God, which resulted from sin, was accompanied immediately by a blight on human fellowship also. Bickering and passing the blame broke out at once between Adam and Eve, and the antagonism of their sons resulted in murder. We will not fully understand our problems in human relationships until we see them as the expression of the active rebellion and independency which has afflicted human nature.

A vast arsenal of weapons against human fellowship

grows out of this source. Fear, anger, jealousy, envy, bitterness, revenge, flattery, accusation, and many other injurious conditions develop from the sickness of a human nature estranged from God and trying unsuccessfully to defend its own "god-status" against all comers.

Christ, in healing the breach between us and God and enabling us to walk again in fellowship with Him, was also dealing with the root of bitterness among human beings. He redeemed our human relationships with the very same stroke that healed our separation from God.

It is a mistake to assume that all human disabilities are to be removed from our lives during this present earthly life—that this is what our Christian faith is designed to do for us. But it is an even greater mistake to underestimate the healing power of fellowship with God. What we need in the way of a growing mental, emotional, and volitional health, which in turn will provide healing for human relationships, is directly associated with the spiritual dynamics of intimacy with God. Our progress toward powerful lives, healed marriages, strong fellowship in worship and prayer, the experience of burden-bearing and mutual encouragement, and the sharing of love is to be found in this.

By now it should be clear that we are not talking about fellowship on a superficial level. Rather we are talking about the profound effects of God's presence with his people. We are talking about an intimate connection with God, a basic healing of life that comes about increasingly as the negative dynamics of independency are overcome and the healing presence of the Spirit of God is at work in us and our human relationships as well.

This is really what Christianity is about.

TWO

The Role of Scripture

An understanding of the true role of Scripture is probably more central to a profitable understanding of spiritual dynamics than any other single factor. What you do with the scriptural content of this book will determine in large measure how it affects your life, how much it enlarges your fellowship with God, and how much it promotes your experience of redemptive power.

The Bible deals with truth. Even a person antagonistic to Christianity will usually acknowledge this fact. A Christian immediately wants to say much more than this. However, the fact that the Bible deals with truth has significance in itself. It implies that there is an appeal to the mind of the reader; you've got to put out mental effort if you're going to profit from its statements. There are propositions, logical relationships, and implications to be understood. There are beauties which will only be seen with careful study and much pondering.

This is not to say that the value of Scripture can be received simply by careful study. Other factors will come into play, but this must not obscure the fact that we need a *mental* grasp of God's Word. The Bible is verbal communication of truth. It is an insult to its character to pass over it without careful thought and investigation.

There is power in truth. Simple facts sometimes open up vast new horizons of possibilities and interests to the mind, as the discovery of microorganisms did for medicine. The Bible certainly has this kind of power.

But the unique power of the Bible does not lie only in the fact that it is truth. If this were so, its power would always come from its inherent force. We would examine it as an archaeologist studies an artifact dug from the ground, to see what it has power to reveal about its long-departed maker. We would examine the Bible, for example, to see what principles of guidance God has left us for the living of a righteous life. Its power to influence our lives would come solely from the rightness of these principles in and of themselves. The Bible would be a textbook.

This can be a very attractive idea, especially if we consider the Bible as the complete textbook on *redemptive* ideas: all the data needed for the directing of faith, for understanding the just requirements of God, the sinfulness of man, the work of Christ, the nature of a Christian life style, and so on. And these truths are definitely present with all their intrinsic force.

But the unique power of the Bible lies in the fact that God sovereignly associates Himself with His Word. He reveals Himself by Scripture; he doesn't just issue data about Himself. He actively uses it as His instrument to create a relationship with Himself.

Imagine yourself on a cold day outside a large window. The heat of the room within has steamed up the window, and as you come close, you realize that someone has written with his finger on the inside of the window. You stand there reading what has been printed. Your eyes are focused on the writing. But suddenly you become aware that you can see through the writing to the room beyond, and a person, presumably the writer, is standing immediately behind the window. Your sudden change of attitude is something like what happens as God confronts us with His living presence when we thought we were just looking at the words of Scripture.

Hebrews 4:12, 13 describes this very experience. Verse 12 says, "The word of God is living and active. Sharper than any double-edged sword, it penetrates even to dividing soul and spirit, joints and marrow; it judges the thoughts and attitudes of the heart" (NIV). The emphasis is on "it," the Word of God, and on what is indeed the intrinsic power of its truth. But suddenly the perspective changes in verse 13, and an awesome reality emerges: "Nothing in all creation is hidden from *God's sight.* Everything is uncovered and laid bare before the eyes of him to whom we must give account" (italics added). As the Word is confronting us with *its* standards and truth, we become aware that we are actually under the scrutiny of the living God! God is confronting us with Himself!

All truth has some measure of intrinsic power. The Holy Spirit is certainly the Spirit of truth and in some way stands behind all truth. But the manner in which God accompanies His Word with His own redemptive presence and power makes its function unique among literary productions. It becomes an instrument of dynamic effectiveness as He wields it. Amazing and powerful things happen! It is an essential ingredient of spiritual dynamics.

We must understand that in associating Himself with His Word, in using it as His powerful instrument of grace, God in no way limits His sovereignty or power of choice. God is not imprisoned in His truth so that the impact of Scripture comes automatically on all persons who are exposed to it. He wields it as He wills. We see the effects multiply in the heart of that person in whom He has chosen to work. In the following paragraphs we shall look at some of the powerful events that take place as the living God accompanies and uses His Word.

One of the important effects of the association of God with His Word is the authenticating of the Word itself. The Apostle Paul described the coming of the gospel to the Thessalonians in these words: "Our Gospel came to you not simply with words, but also with power, with the Holy Spirit and with deep conviction . . . you welcomed the message with the joy given by the Holy Spirit . . . when you received the word of God, which you heard from us, you accepted it not as the word of men, but as it actually is, the word of God, which is at work in you who believe" (1 Thess. 1:5, 6; 2:13, NIV). *The Westminster Confession of Faith* (I:5) states this principle. The testimony of the Church, the nature of the Word itself, and the effects that it can produce tend to create "a high and reverent esteem for the Holy Scripture" and constitute evidence that it is the Word of God. "Yet, notwithstanding," it goes on, "our full persuasion of the infallible truth and divine authority thereof, is from the inward work of the Holy Spirit, bearing witness by and with the word in our hearts" (I:5). Whether it comes with the simple preaching of the gospel or by means of more comprehensive study of Scripture, wherever the Holy Spirit is initiating or carrying on a work of grace in a person's heart, He accompanies the communication of truth with an authenticating witness. A firm assurance is born concerning the reliability of the message.

Parents trust that the testimony they (along with the larger Church) have given to their children concerning the Bible will be enough to make an attitude of submission to it permanent. They are often deeply grieved and perplexed to discover, when the children are older, that "full assurance of its infallible truth and divine authority" was not produced and maintained that way. The testimony of parents and Church surely must be given, but the added dimension of the Holy Spirit's witness "by and with the Word in their hearts" is the ultimate essential.

The Holy Spirit has been providing this kind of powerful, authenticating witness along with Scripture throughout many centuries of theological ups and downs in the Church. If we were to comprehend more fully His marvelous power and constant activity in this process, we might face times of doctrinal instability with less fear. The evangelical cause is not automatically lost when it becomes weak in its doctrine of Scripture; indeed, the tide will eventually turn because of this activity of the Spirit.

A special application of this authenticating witness of the Spirit of God which accompanies Scripture was involved in the process by which the Church discerned which writings actually belonged in the Bible and which did not. The fact that a prevailing majority of Christians was able to sense which writings were authentically inspired bears witness to the reality of this work of God's Spirit.

Similar to the authenticating witness of the Holy Spirit is the way He accompanies the Word with His teaching ministry. To say that no one can really be sure how to interpret the Bible is to ignore the reality of God's hand upon His Word. The Holy Spirit is indeed the "anointing that teaches" (cf. 1 John 2:20, 27).

This does not mean at all that we are exempt from careful study of the Bible. Nor does it mean that we will have no need to grasp relationships between the various parts of divine revelation or use good principles of interpretation. It does not mean that He has no use for human instruments to aid in such studies. But it does mean that we are ultimately dependent on the Holy Spirit's help for understanding the Word, and that this assistance is real and trustworthy.

Here again, He is sovereign in the way He teaches. He is God, and works where and when He will. We may invoke Him—we may ask Him for this gracious ministry—but it is never automatically associated with the truth. He is no prisoner of His Word.

Still another amazing effect of God's accompanying His Word is the creation of life. Spiritual death is a significant concept in the Bible. The Genesis account records it as the promised consequence of the first disobedience: "From the tree of the knowledge of good and evil you shall not eat, for in the day that you eat from it you shall surely die" (Gen. 2:17, NASB). It seems clear that this means more than physical death. Physical death was not an immediate result of the disobedience. Rather a spiritual separation from the life of God and destruction of close fellowship with Him were the immediate consequences. This initial tragedy then became the universal experience of mankind: ". . . sin entered the world through one man, and death through sin, and in this way death came to all men . . ." (Rom. 5:12, NIV).

The remarkable thing about Scripture is not merely its teaching that spiritual life must be imparted to spiritually dead sinners, but its own agency in creating that life. Somehow, in our confrontation with the living God through the Word, life itself is generated. This is the teaching of a profound sentence from James: "He chose to give us birth through the word of truth, that we might be a kind of firstfruits of all he created" (James 1:18, NIV). The sovereign choice of God is in view here—His own creative power displayed in the gift of spiritual life. But most astonishing is His choice to do this by the agency of the word of truth.

Closely associated with the gift of life is the gift of faith through the agency of the Word. The Bible, as part of its revelation of data about God, makes plain that faith in God is essential to the establishment of a relationship with Him: "Without faith it is impossible to please God, because anyone who comes to him must believe that he exists and that he rewards those who earnestly seek him" (Heb. 11:6, NIV). But the Word does more than this. Somehow, in the vital confrontation that takes place when the Spirit of God is sovereignly using Scripture, there comes the actual creation of faith. To Timothy, Paul says, "From infancy you have known the holy Scriptures, which are able [have power] to make you wise for salvation through faith in Christ Jesus" (2 Tim. 3:15, NIV). While the power of Scripture is clearly in view here, faith is stated as an indirect consequence of the process. In Romans, Paul puts it more directly: "So faith comes from hearing, and hearing by the word of Christ" (Rom. 10:17, NASB). The New English Bible at this point has an intriguing paraphrase: "We conclude that faith is awakened by the message, and the message that awakens it comes through the word of Christ." In any case, the agency of the word or message in producing faith is clear.

In each of these latter passages, there is emphasis on the fact that Jesus Christ is the central focus of the biblical message. It is especially noteworthy that Paul's word to Timothy refers to the capacity of *Old Testament* Scriptures to arouse wisdom and faith directed toward Christ. There is an overall sense, then, in which *any* portion of Scripture is related to the common Christ-centered thrust of all Scripture, and so instructs us about Him.

But again, the gospel is more than simply a message about Christ, just as surely as it is more than merely a message about faith. The living Christ occupies a much closer relationship to the gospel than that. Two passages from Paul's letter to the Ephesians show that *Christ brings the message Himself*—that He Himself is the Evangelist.

The first of these passages is in Ephesians 2, where Paul describes the redemptive work of Christ in healing the breach between Jews and Gentiles. He speaks of Christ as having done this personally by His own death and resurrection. Then, exactly at this point in the redemption sequence, verse 17 tells us: "*And he came* and preached peace to you who were far away, and peace to those who were near" (NASB, italics added). This is the approach of the risen Christ—Christ the Evangelist. It is literally a case of Christ accompanying the gospel with his personal presence, of Christ offering Himself in the gospel.

In Ephesians 4, Paul exhorts Christians to take note of the spiritual condition of non-Christian Gentiles, who are callous and given over to the practice of all kinds of evil. Then come these words: "But you did not learn Christ in this way, if indeed *you have heard him* and have been taught in [by] him, just as the truth is in Jesus" (Eph. 4:20, 21, NASB, italics added). The concept of the living Christ speaking the message to the hearer's heart is a radical and powerful one. It is regrettable that many modern translations fail to catch the force of this idea. Where the original Greek has a direct object: "you heard *him*," RSV has "you have heard about him"; NEB: "were you not told of him"; and NIV: "Surely you heard of him." Phillips catches the true impact of it: "But you have learned nothing like that from Christ, if you have really heard his voice and understood the truth that Jesus has taught you."

It is no great leap of understanding to realize that the aim of Christ's confronting the hearer with Himself, as He accompanies the Word, is to encourage a personal relationship with Himself. He intends so much more than merely to gain our acquiescence to objective truth about Himself. The goal is a faith which embraces His Person and what He has done; the goal is real fellowship with Christ. The advice sometimes given to unbelievers to "let Jesus come into your heart" is more than a way of speaking to children. It is the way of the gospel and the way of salvation. The authors of the Westminster standards apparently had this in mind when they described effectual calling in these terms: " . . . the work of God's Spirit, whereby, convincing us of our sin and misery, enlightening our minds in the knowledge of Christ, and renewing our wills, he doth persuade and enable us *to embrace Jesus Christ* freely offered to us in the gospel" (Westminster Shorter Catechism, Question 31, italics added).

Scripture has still another way of describing this reality—this time involving the third person of the Trinity. Twice in Galatians 3, Paul asks an important question of his readers. Verse 2: "Received ye the Spirit by the works of the law, or by the hearing of faith?" And again in verse 5: "He therefore that ministereth to you [provides] the Spirit, and worketh miracles among you, doeth he it by the works of the law, or by the hearing of faith?" (KJV). "The hearing of faith" (a valuable reading from the King James) apparently describes the same phenomenon that we have been discussing. The word of truth, the gospel, accompanied by a sovereign work of authentication, the gift of life, and faith in Christ results in establishing a personal relationship with the Spirit of God.

What we have been describing in the preceding paragraphs underscores the reason why the gospel is called by Paul "the word of reconciliation" (2 Cor. 5:19, NASB). We have noted that fellowship between God and His human creatures is basic to His design. For us to love Him with all our being is His greatest expectation and desire of us. It is the great commandment. Scripture is God's instrument to create fellowship with Him. Not at all content merely to reveal data about Himself, He confronts us with Himself. And in this confrontation lies the potential for establishing or enlarging a deep and personal relationship between us and Him.

Whether, then, we talk of God in terms of the Father, or the Son, or the Holy Spirit—His deep desire to be known and loved, to have fellowship with His human creatures, comes to expression in the dynamic way he uses His Word. He personally accompanies it and draws the hearer to Himself. Involved will be a necessary authentication of the message, the awakening of spiritual life, the hearing of faith, the embracing of Christ, and the very presence of God's Spirit in the heart. He is the Person behind the window, focusing our attention upon Himself by His Word and bringing to bear on us the necessary power to set up and develop our relationship with Him. Until we see this and become thoroughly aware of this role of Scripture, we have not understood the real use of the Word.

Such an understanding of the role of Scripture will strengthen and somewhat modify our reasons for contending for the integrity of the whole Bible. If this is the instrument God uses to lead us into fellowship with Himself, if its sufficiency lies in the fact that there He has revealed all truth necessary to establish, build, and maintain that fellowship, then we do not want to lose one iota of the instrument. We will deeply desire to conserve Scripture, not because we are conservative and traditional by nature and find our security in being that way about everything, but *because of the very strength of our desire to know God!* If the instrument is having its designed effect, and fellowship with God is being enlarged, we may become anything but conservative in other matters! We will rather be concerned to be on the cutting edge of whatever our living Lord is doing. He may indeed lead us to challenge the status quo in many situations.

This is both a liberating and dangerous concept. It indeed has the potential for liberating us from the deadness which is produced by lesser approaches to Scripture. It must never, however, become an excuse to act in ways that are contrary to Scripture, as though having once been brought to God by the Word we can then discard it while we enjoy sweet fellowship with the Lord. The Scriptures are always to be there, establishing, building, maintaining, and *measuring* our walk with God.

There are many practical ways in which this understanding of the Bible's role should shape our approach to it. For one thing, the Bible deserves earnest and careful study. When we say that the whole message of the Bible centers in the person and work of Jesus Christ, this lays on us a continuous task of discovering these connections, understanding relationships, comparing and reinterpreting data, as the unity of Scripture comes more into focus. As we said earlier, we are dealing with truth, and our minds must of necessity be engaged.

There is also a clear need to bring prayer to the study of Scripture. We will need to pray much for the work of the Holy Spirit in illuminating and applying Scripture to our hearts. We must not let the idea of

God's sovereignty keep us from requesting His work in our behalf! We have made a poor start indeed in understanding the Bible if we do not realize that the sovereign God urges us often to ask Him for His works. If we are believers in Christ, we start with the assurance that He has already chosen to use His Word in our hearts to produce life and faith. We are right to believe that "he who began a good work in you will carry it on to completion until the day of Jesus Christ" (Phil. 1:6, NIV). His sovereign choices will be shown in the selective way He applies the Word to the exact places where He desires us to grow.

Strongly present in our approach to Scripture should be the desire and expectation to meet God through it. Here is where merely academic study of the Bible can be dangerous. If it is truly the design of God to build our fellowship with the Lord Himself through the Word, we should always be ready to respond to Him as instructed by Scripture. To be only building our store of knowledge without responding personally to Him is to become increasingly sterile and lifeless in our spiritual tone—actually made so by our misuse of the Bible! Let us rather, when the Spirit of truth opens up biblical material in such a way as to convince us of sin, freely respond to the Lord in confession and repentance. When we grasp something more clearly of His nature and works, let us come back to Him with praise and thanksgiving. When some response of faith toward Christ is indicated as central to our walk with Him, let us make that response in prayer. When we become aware of a promise of God in the Word that clearly applies to our situation, let us come to Him with a claim of faith built on that promise.

Form the habit of approaching the Bible or sermons built on the Bible or any other vehicle by which biblical truth is brought to you—including this book—with the expectation that the living God will confront you personally and teach you the appropriate responses of faith to make to Him on the basis of those truths. In this way your fellowship with Him will be continually enlarged and made more intelligent and effective as you give attention to His message. Do not imagine that you can make continuing progress in your experience of fellowship with God without this function of the Word of God in your life!

The Creature Problem

The next four chapters will consider the question: Why is it difficult to walk in fellowship with God? Christian teaching has commonly organized negative dynamics under the familiar headings of the world, the flesh, and the devil; but to these three we are adding the subject of the present chapter—the problem of our creaturehood.

Previously discussed was the design of God to create beings with a personality structure capable of interacting with Himself. This emphasized the positive likenesses shared by God and human beings. There are, however, also large differences. In light of these, it is really astounding that we are talking at all about interaction between finite and limited beings on the one hand, and an infinite and unlimited Being on the other. The thought of fellowship between those who are both material and spiritual beings, on the one hand, and one who is pure spirit, on the other, is especially significant.

The pattern of God's creative activity at once suggests God's own involvement and concern over the material/spiritual distinction. Six days He involved Himself in the labors of creating the material universe and the inhabitants of earth. But on the seventh day He rested from His work and set apart that day as having peculiar significance for human kind (Gen. 2:1-3). The length of these "days" is not the important thing for us here. Rather it is the pattern of involvement in the material creation followed by a "rest" from that involvement.

Jesus taught that the Sabbath was "made for man" (Mark 2:27, KJV), by this implying that it was designed to meet a created need in this material/spiritual being. Something of the pattern of God's own on-and-off involvement with material creation would be essential to mankind also.

When the Genesis Sabbath-thought is next picked up in Scripture, it is on the occasion of the first giving of manna to the children of Israel in the wilderness. Exodus 16 records Moses' words: "Tomorrow is to be a day of rest, a holy Sabbath to the Lord. . . . Bear in mind that the Lord has given you the Sabbath" (verses 23, 29, NIV). These thoughts were amplified in the Sabbath commandment: "Remember the Sabbath day by keeping it holy. Six days you shall labor and do all your work, but the seventh day is a Sabbath to the Lord your God" (Ex. 20:8-10, NIV). Besides stating the thought which Jesus later echoed, that the Sabbath was a gift for man's benefit, these passages make plain that it is to be a period of time dedicated in some unique way *to the Lord.*

The Old Testament makes it plain that for the godly person of that era, just as for godly persons of any era, all activities are to be carried out with an eye toward God. "In all your ways acknowledge him [literally, know him], and he will make your paths straight" (Prov. 3:6, NIV). Yet this will not be enough! Human beings need to stop their involvement in physical/material pursuits and devote significant periods of time to the Lord in a regular, recurring cycle. The implication is that our creaturely involvement in the task of dominating the earth can stifle our spiritual awareness and cause a withering of that side of our nature. Our contemplative capacity, our occupation with true worship, will need special and undistracted exercise.

So the Sabbath was God's gift to mankind to enable us to keep the two sides of our nature in balance. The fact that the Sabbath later came under the Mosaic legal structure, and that later still this dimension was in some way altered under the New Covenant, in no way changes the basic principle. Human nature needed this gift from creation on, even before sin entered the scene. Under grace we still have this created need. A delicate balance is required to know how to meet our need for Sabbath rest without descending from grace to legalism.

A scriptural view of fasting may well place it in the same category as Sabbath observance, although at a more intensive level. In Old Testament times fasts were called on occasions of public calamities, afflictions, or approaching danger. They were also observed in connection with bereavement and mourning, or with a need for direction or protection. Fasting involves the same discontinuing of normal occupations in the material/physical sphere, but with the accent on withdrawal from food. The important thing is that fasting, like Sabbath observance, was to be "to the Lord." It was a time for seeking Him: His solace, His protection, His favor and guidance. This note is caught in the following expression from Ezra: "There, by the Ahava Canal, I proclaimed a fast, so that we might humble ourselves before our God and ask him for a safe journey for us and our children, with all of our possessions. . . . So we fasted and petitioned our God about this, and he answered our prayer" (Ezra 8:21, 23, NIV). Through the prophet Zechariah, God asks, "When ye fasted and mourned in the fifth and seventh month, even those seventy years, did ye at all fast unto me, even to me?" (Zech. 7:5, KJV).

The extent of our need for a Sabbath rest is emphasized by what the Bible means by *godliness* and *ungodliness*. The root of the Greek word conveyed the original idea of "falling back" in awe. It came to be a word frequently used for worship and the acts of worship. In its New Testament usage, it refers to a reverential awareness of God, an awareness that conditions a person's actions. It is startling to realize what the Bible means when it says that God's wrath "is revealed from heaven against all ungodliness and unrighteousness of men" (Rom. 1:18, NASB). The words *ungodliness* and *unrighteousness* are not synonyms. *Unrighteousness* refers to the violation of God's standards. But *ungodliness* refers to a lack of reverential awareness of God.

It is quite possible to be doing nothing overtly wicked and yet be ungodly. One can be orthodox, evangelical, even actively defending the faith, and be ungodly in the process. One can be engaging in prescribed acts of worship, or be preaching an expository sermon which is true to the doctrines of Scripture, and at the same time be ungodly. The point of Romans 1:18 is that ungodliness is just as distressing to God as acts of transgression. For He is a God who desires to be *known* for who He is—known and loved with all our heart and strength.

How then *does* one keep the Sabbath principle today? Without being legalistic, we can certainly realize the need to have periods of time—long or short—during which we discontinue our involvement in the earthbound side of life and devote full attention to God. Times spent carefully in private devotions are in this sense a fulfillment of the Sabbath principle. So also are periods of family worship. Moments spent in quiet contemplation and worship might well be sprinkled through our activities and bring God-ward meaning to them. The old farmer who would drive his horse and plow to the edge of the field, pause with bowed head, and say, "In the name of God, we begin," was doing this. Obviously, times spent assembling with God's people for attendance on the Word and for worship provide opportunities for Sabbath keeping, although they may be used in such a manner that they miss being *genuine* Sabbath keeping. Fasting certainly can still be a legitimate and more intensive way of devoting attention to the Lord, so long as it does not become a work by which we expect to merit God's blessing or avert His displeasure.

It is characteristic of Americans, and characteristic of the age, that we are caught up in an overwhelming preoccupation with the pragmatic, the mundane, the physical. We have lost the contemplative art! Robert Louis Stevenson said that some people have not one thought to rub against another while waiting for the train. Never was there a day when it was more needful to rediscover the blessing of Sabbath observance without the curse of legalism.

One result of our lack in this regard is a vulnerability to the sensational in matters connected with God. There are indeed many occasions when God sovereignly displays His power in the sphere of our senses. It is marvelous, and worthy of much praise, when a miracle alters the ordinary course of nature in a way that we can apprehend with our senses. But if we are neglecting the development of our spiritual fellowship with a spiritual God, we can come to count on these miraculous interventions as our most real acquaintance with God, our most genuine contact with Him. As this takes place, we more and more minimize the need for the other development. Quite apart from the merits of phenomena like tongues-speaking, healings, visions, and being "slain by the Spirit," the involvement of Christians in these experiences carries with it the danger of spiritual atrophy. The God who really *is* may become increasingly strange to us, even in the midst of His miraculous activity!

Mark this well: You may know all there is to know from Scripture and from experience about sin and its motions, about the devil and his attacks, about the subtle snares of this world, and even know all the spiritual dynamics discussed in this book and more. But if you do not take time apart to cultivate godliness, you will find it hard to walk in fellowship with God. True observance of the Sabbath principle must become part of your life style.

The service of your will in choosing to set apart times for God and disciplining your walk to keep them is not necessarily legalism, but can be an essential part of the operation of grace. "The fruit of the Spirit is . . . self-control" (Gal. 5:22, 23, NIV).

FOUR

The Flesh

"Sin entered the world through one man, and death through sin" (Rom. 5:12, NIV). Its presence can severely hurt our fellowship with God. That's why a study of the dynamics of sin is important for understanding the dynamics of intimacy with God.

The Bible uses the word *sin* to describe actions that are contrary to God's righteous expectations. But it is crucial to our study to recognize that Scripture also uses *sin* to describe an inner affliction of human nature. This dual use is suggested, for example, in 1 John 1:8, 10, where in the first instance the text reads, "If we say that we have no sin, we are deceiving ourselves," and in the second, "If we say that we have not sinned, we make him a liar" (NASB). The expression "to *have* sin" describes an affliction of our nature.

Jesus spoke of this inward condition as the actual source of outward acts of sin: "What comes out of a man is what makes him 'unclean.' For from within, out of men's hearts, come evil thoughts, sexual immorality, theft, murder, adultery, greed, malice, deceit, lewdness, envy, slander, arrogance and folly. All these evils come from inside and make a man 'unclean' " (Mark 7:20-23, NIV).

Perhaps the definitive treatment of sin in human nature is the Apostle Paul's use of the term *the flesh* (Greek, *sarx*). While modern translations use a variety of expressions for this word, we shall use the word *flesh* partly for the sake of consistency, and also because it is part of the classical trio of opponents to a Christian's walk: "the world, the flesh, and the devil." In the whole of Scripture, *flesh* appears fairly frequently and with a variety of meanings. In Paul's writings, however, he invests it with an increasingly sharp meaning, which becomes apparent in several strategic passages.

Romans 8:2, 3 makes plain the connection in Paul's thought between *sin* and *the flesh:* "For the law of the Spirit of life in Christ Jesus has set you free from the law of sin and of death. For what the Law could not do, weak as it was through the flesh, God did: sending his own Son in the likeness of sinful flesh and as an offering for sin, he condemned sin in the flesh" (NASB). The meaning for *flesh* in this passage which makes the most sense is quite simply "faulty human nature." Paul considers our nature to have been corrupted by the presence of sin. It is "sinful flesh," and he speaks of "sin in the flesh." The Son took on Himself human nature in order that the sin which resides in human nature might be judged in Him.

This idea of *the flesh* as synonymous with corrupted human nature is strongly supported by Paul's testimony about himself in Philippians 3:3-6: "For it is we who are the circumcision, we who worship by the Spirit of God, who glory in Christ Jesus, and who put no confidence in the flesh—though I myself have reasons for such confidence. If anyone else thinks he has reasons to put confidence in the flesh, I have more: circumcised on the eighth day, of the people of Israel, of the tribe of Benjamin, a Hebrew of the Hebrews; in regard to the law, a Pharisee; as for zeal, persecuting the church; as for legalistic righteousness, faultless" (NIV). Paul seems to include under the term *flesh* everything that he personally was—by heredity, enculturation, education, circumstances, and personality—even religious characteristics. He indicates that in his own case these attributes would ordinarily be considered superior to most, yet says that as a Christian his outlook on his personality is that it is fatally flawed and untrustworthy.

This passage makes it plain that *lower nature* in the New English Bible is an inadequate and misleading translation for *sarx*. The influence and presence of sin conditions all parts of human nature, "higher" or "lower," and makes it all untrustworthy when the personality is functioning according to its unaided nature.

"Sinful human nature" is what Paul means by *flesh*. But Romans 8:6, 7 gives a significant understanding of the nature of this sinfulness. Twice in these verses an unusual Greek word is used in association with *sarx*. A simple translation in each case would be "the *mind* of the flesh." It is a rare form, however, appearing only in this chapter of the New Testament. Used to describe the mind, it gives the idea of the *tendency* or *disposition* of the mind, or more strongly, the *direction*, the *aim*, the *striving*, or the *bent* of the mind. Note, then, the two statements that are made concerning the *flesh* in these verses. First, "the direction, or aim, or *bent* of mind of the flesh is death"; second, "the direction, or aim, or bent of mind of the flesh is enmity toward God. For to the law of God it does not subject itself, for it is not able to" (expanded translation). Sin in human nature is shaped toward death, because it strives to be independent of God. It strives toward autonomy, and this tendency is so deeply ingrained, so antagonistic toward the rule of God, that it cannot tolerate the idea of submission. It is powerless to do so.

It is scriptural and accurate to call this sin of human nature, this shaping or striving of the flesh, a *god-complex*. In fact, Satan's earliest approach to mankind held out the prospect that disobedience would make them "like God," or even "like gods" (Gen. 3:5). In other words, he held out to them the prospect of achieving some measure of God-status which had to that point been denied them. Both Scripture and experience teach us how strongly the love for autonomy has gripped human thinking. We want the prerogatives of God; this is now the deep drive of our nature.

Human nature has become sensitive to everything that might threaten its assumed "god-rights." Most significantly this applies to thoughts about God Himself.

Romans 1:28 states this in a striking way: "Since they did not think it worthwhile to retain the knowledge of God, he gave them over to a depraved mind, to do what ought not to be done" (NIV). What the Apostle Paul literally says here is that man tested and rejected the idea of knowing God accurately, whereupon God tested and rejected man's mind as worthless. The result was an outpouring of evil. But why should mankind have rejected an accurate knowledge of God, except that this would cut into his own autonomy? After having once tasted the intoxicating thrill of independence, man found this unthinkable.

Understanding this dimension of sinful human nature adds much to our concept of ungodliness. Ungodliness is the lack of a reverential awareness of God; but that is only its passive side. It also involves an active hostility toward the awareness of God which is bred by the protection of its own supposed rights.

The sensitivity that human beings have toward anything threatening their autonomy not only involves them in hostility toward God and His rights, but also toward the threat posed by other human beings. In ways that can be enormously complicated, we defend our independent status and security from each other. The flesh not only sees the true and living God as a threat to its self-rule and independence, but encounters a world full of people driven by the same god-complex and therefore posing a similar threat. We fear the possibility of being tyrannized, exploited, harmed, or curbed in our independence by one another!

We should see this characteristic of our nature as the exact antithesis of God's design for fellowship between man and Himself, and among human beings. Enmity, indifference, isolation hold the field against love.

The independency of the flesh permeates and blights all the characteristic functions of personality. It becomes a strong drive in the rational processes, expressing itself in the tendency to trust one's own reasoning, set up one's own unaided mind as judge of truth, allow whatever fantasy-thinking is pleasurable to one's self, and defend one's own thought against all threats from God or man. This does not mean that sinful people never think truth or use their minds in relatively good or fruitful ways. The grace of God is exhibited much in human thinking, with many brilliant indications of the sheer magnitude of this human capacity. God also sovereignly uses the thoughts of men to serve His purposes. The minds of kings can be turned in whatever way He desires. Nevertheless, if "good" is ultimately defined to include godliness as well as righteousness, no thinking is finally good that does not proceed in fellowship with God.

Emotional life is deeply affected by the flesh. A tangled mass of fears, hostilities, complexes, longings, passions, and hurts are generated in us toward God and each other by our independency. Again, this does not mean that ungodly people never express emotional reactions that are in some sense good. The emotional capacity also is great. Art and music, by the grace of God, can marvelously display aesthetic excellence, even when produced by otherwise godless people. Even so, ultimate good is absent, and often the very people who have produced these things show deep imbalances in their emotional lives which make them classically tragic figures.

The innate drive for independency and self-protection has its impact on all human functions. The will, sexuality, motivations, social and group functions, indeed all areas of life, are touched. All parts and functions of our nature have been affected by this sickness.

Now we must look at a crucial question. How much of a problem is the flesh to Christians? If we have been correct in isolating the basic problem of human nature as its drive toward autonomy and independence, it would seem that the process of becoming a Christian would make profound changes that would alleviate, or even remove, this problem. Is it not true that the gospel is a word of reconciliation to God, and the means of restoring fellowship with Him? Is it not true that the Holy Spirit takes up residence in the believer at the time of his conversion? Is it not true that for the Christian, *life* has replaced the isolation of death, that "old things have passed away, and all things have become new" (2 Cor. 5:17, KJV)?

The direction in which the answer to this question lies is immediately suggested by the fact that Paul uses the concept of the flesh most often in connection with explanations and exhortations made to Christians. The passage containing Paul's testimony about his own background begins with the general statement that

Christians are those "who put no confidence in the flesh" (Phil. 3:3, NIV). In itself this statement might be taken to mean that Christians do not trust human nature in non-Christian people. Paul goes on, however, to expose the temptation it would be to him to trust his own flesh, and the strong hunger that he has as a Christian to learn to live another way. No, Christians are those who ought to have learned to distrust *their own* sinful nature. This is the clear impact of this passage.

Surprising as it may seem that Christians *still* have a problem with their flesh, it is strongly confirmed by Paul's exhortation to the Galatian Christians: "You were called to freedom, brethren; only do not turn your freedom into an opportunity for the flesh, but through love serve one another. . . . Walk by the Spirit, and you will not carry out the desire of the flesh. For the flesh sets its desire against the Spirit, and the Spirit against the flesh; for these are in opposition to one another, so that you may not do the things that you please. . . . The one who sows to his own flesh shall from the flesh reap corruption, but the one who sows to the Spirit shall from the Spirit reap eternal life" (Gal. 5:13, 16, 17; 6:8, NASB).

The warnings of this section of Scripture show unmistakably that Christians still have the problem of the flesh. A life style in which the flesh at times predominates is a distinct possibility for believers. The expression of Galatians 5:17 that the flesh "sets its desire against the Spirit" sounds very much as though the drive for personal sovereignty creates strong conflict between the Christian and the indwelling Spirit of God. The Apostle does not here speak of the flesh as though it is a weakened characteristic, now feebly struggling against the motions of the Holy Spirit. Nor is it described in terms that would suggest that it is now but a lower part of our nature which struggles against a higher part. Our confidence as Christians does not rest in the fact that we are now inherently *better* than we were, although our situation has indeed drastically improved, but in the fact that the almighty Spirit of God is now present with us, warring against the flesh, encouraging new motives and desires, and creating new possibilities for us.

A sense of conflict is prominent in Romans 7: "The Law is spiritual; but I am of flesh, sold into bondage to sin. . . . I am not practicing what I would like to do, but I am doing the very thing that I hate. . . . So now, no longer am I the one doing it, but sin which indwells me. For I know that nothing good dwells in me, that is, in my flesh; for the wishing is present with me, but the doing of the good is not. . . . I find then the principle that evil is present with me, the one who wishes to do good. For I joyfully concur with the Law of God in the inner man, but I see a different law in the members of my body, waging war against the law of my mind, and making me a prisoner of the law of sin which is in my members. Wretched man that I am! Who will set me free from the body of this death?" (Rom 7:14, 15, 17, 18, 21-24, NASB). Many feel that such a picture of conflict and wretchedness compels one to interpret this entire passage as descriptive of a non-Christian. Exactly the reverse is true. The motions toward righteousness that Paul expresses here are the motions of a spiritually awakened man. He has actually come to hate sin and evil and to desire with great intensity to do good. He has, however, awakened also to the reality of the flesh and its strong bent against the Spirit. No one but a Christian can be so keenly aware of the wretchedness of such a conflict.

What these passages teach us powerfully is that the flesh, with its drive toward independence and its reactions to anything that might threaten its assumed rights, is still a real factor in a Christian's experience. Its power is such that it sometimes can very nearly drive sincere Christians to despair in the early stages of their Christian lives, and to a hardening skepticism in later stages.

New Testament teaching is plain in this area. The Bible nowhere teaches that the sinful character of human nature is removed at conversion, nor even in the processes of Christian growth. As long as we are in these bodies, we are taught that we "who have the firstfruits of the Spirit, groan inwardly as we wait eagerly for our adoption as sons, the redemption of our bodies" (Rom. 8:23, NIV). Taken in connection with other passages, these verses clearly indicate that Paul is not here teaching that matter (in this case, the human body) is in itself evil and therefore the source of our problem. Rather, the teaching is that so long as we are in this present bodily existence, human nature still carries its sinful affliction and pressures us away from God. How amazing that the Holy Spirit of God takes up intimate residence in the believer despite it all!

Much indeed changes for us as soon as we open our hearts to Christ! There is new life, the passing from darkness to light, forgiveness, acceptance with God, rescue from the kingdom of Satan, the presence of the Holy Spirit in our lives. But none of these changes means that God has taken from us in this life the powerful drive of the flesh. It is there and must be reckoned with. Its dynamic is strong; but in finding a superior power by which to conquer the drive of the flesh, Christians bear a kind of testimony to a watching world. We could never be so effective if we were not still cut from the same piece of damaged cloth as the rest of humanity.

In the preceding chapter the comment was made that it is quite possible for us to be ungodly even while doing things that are outwardly good—that is, to operate without a reverential awareness of, and fellowship with, our God. It now may be seen that this is precisely what our sinful nature desires. Subtly and strongly the push of our flesh toward independence can creep into the most "holy" of activities and create ungodliness. Yet we are so accustomed to assessing sinfulness only in terms of unrighteous deeds, that we will seldom with equal alarm label ungodliness as sin.

This is where we need insight. Until we recognize the sheer strength of sin operating in our nature, the subtlety of its drive for independence from God, and the bitterness of the fruit that the flesh produces, we will never be realistic in our search for the power of Christ. We will tend to content ourselves with passive concepts like "surrendering ourselves to Christ," without taking hold of the true dynamics of Christianity to deal with our problem and make submission possible.

FIVE

Satan

According to the Bible, the human problem of rebellion and independency is associated with and aggravated by the activity of Satan. There is both a history and a current reality to this. If we are to be thorough and realistic in assessing why it is difficult to walk in fellowship with God, we must understand Satan's role in the problem.

Both Old and New Testaments help us here. At the outset of the Old Testament, Genesis introduces an agent of temptation in the account of man's original fall: "Now the serpent was more crafty than any of the wild animals the Lord God had made. He said to the woman, 'Did God really say. . . ?' " (Gen. 3:1, NIV). Before sin and death became realities to mankind, evil was already operating through the serpent. We might well ask about this shadowy figure, "But who are you, and how does it happen that you are operating this way?"

Particularly in the Old Testament writings, it is important to understand that revelation is progressive. Some find it tempting to say that the Bible merely reflects the current state of human ideas about God and other matters, with little relation to reality. So-called "spiritual-beings" have their only reality in the needs and ideas of the human mind, according to this view. A true view of Scripture acknowledges rather that objective spiritual beings have existed all the time, whether God, angels, Satan, or evil spirits. The scriptural description of these realities, however, starts from a point where nothing previously has been revealed and builds continuously on itself. This is strikingly true of the development of revelation about Satan.

The description of angels develops dramatically in the Old Testament. The early parts of the Bible present them as a kind of extension of the operating power of God, without independent activity, difference of rank, or individual identity. They appear, for example, in the story of Jacob's ladder (Gen. 28:12), as God's army (Gen. 32:2-6), or as attendants of God (Deut. 33:2). A notable exception to this is the frequent appearance of the Angel of God, the being who seems to carry the very presence of God to His people. Demons, or evil spirits, are spoken of in this early period in a nonspecific way, as in the prohibitions against necromancy or dealing with "familiar spirits" (Lev. 19:26, 31; 20:6, 27).

As the Old Testament progresses, angels come into clearer focus. There are, for example, interpreting angels (Job 33:23), angels who carry out God's judgments (Ezek. 9), the seraphim of Isaiah 6. Finally, in the Book of Daniel, specific angels are named (Michael and Gabriel).

A gradual enlargement of God's revelation occurs also with respect to evil spirit beings. To Saul the king comes "an evil spirit from the Lord" (1 Sam. 16:14) to afflict him. Later in the Old Testament we are permitted to see such beings as the "prince of Persia" and the "prince of Grecia," who apparently were high ranking angelic beings of evil character who stand behind human nations and rulers (Daniel 10:13, 21). The conflict between these beings and the angels Michael and Gabriel constitutes a glimpse into little known events in the spirit realm.

In a similar fashion there is development in the Old Testament use of the word *satan*. It is rarely used in the early books of the Bible, and in each case as a general, descriptive term. In its verb form it meant "to lie in wait," or "to oppose," so the noun described "an adversary" or "opponent." It is used only once in the books of Moses (Num. 22:22), where it refers to the Angel of God, who became "an adversary" in the path of Balaam's ass. When the Philistines went off to war, they refused to take David with them for fear that he would become "an adversary" to them (1 Sam. 29:4). In these cases it is not used of an evil being at all, certainly with no reference to the devil.

Later, however, the word *satan* began to have a consistent usage with a definite article before it: "*the* adversary." This makes it obvious that it was now referring to a specific evil being. So it is in the Book of Job.

There are differing opinions about when to place the writing of Job. Most conservative scholars agree that the *events* described in Job are from a pre-Mosaic era. It is not so easy to place the *writing*. Its style and language, its position in the Hebrew Bible (between Proverbs and the Song of Solomon), and its character as Wisdom literature argue for a time near the period of Solomon, perhaps a bit afterward.

Most translators of Job treat the word *satan* as a proper name. Every instance of its use in Job, however, is with the definite article: "*the* adversary." That this being is indeed the devil is obvious from the way he functions as accuser and oppressor of Job; but at this point he has simply the title "the adversary." The same is true of the way the term is used in Zechariah. On each occasion there, in the account of the accusations being brought against the high priest Joshua, the accuser is called "the adversary." The manner in which God addresses this being and uses this title makes it clear that by now it has nearly achieved the status of a proper name.

The last writings of the Old Testament are the books of Chronicles, Ezra, and Nehemiah. In 1 Chronicles 21, there occurs the one clear Old Testament usage of *satan* as a proper name (see Oehler, *Theology of the Old Testament*, n.d., Zondervan, pp. 448, 449). Here the account of David's sin in numbering Israel is reported in the following way: "Satan rose up against Israel and incited David to take a census of Israel" (1 Chron. 21:1, NIV). The word *satan* has become fully developed, from its beginnings as an indefinite expression, "an adversary," with no reference to the devil; then as a title for him, "the adversary"; and finally as his proper name, *Satan.*

There is a distinct possibility that the Old Testament reveals something of the origin of Satan and the history of his adversary character. Almost contemporary with Daniel's prophecy, where we noted the revelation of specific angelic princes standing behind world powers, come the writings of Isaiah and Ezekiel. In these two prophecies occur a pair of remarkable utterances of God. Each of these writers records judgments of the Lord against prominent world powers. Isaiah 14 contains one against the ruler of Babylon, while Ezekiel 28 focuses on the king of Tyre.

In each case, the prophecy is directed against a human king. In each of them, however, there comes a point where there is a change of tone; the language escalates dramatically, and the thoughts expressed become difficult to associate with human beings. In the Isaiah passage the change occurs at verse twelve, and these are the words that follow: "How are you fallen from heaven, O morning star, son of the dawn! You have been cast down to the earth, you who once laid low the nations! You said in your heart, I will ascend to heaven; I will raise my throne above the stars of God; I will sit enthroned on the mount of assembly, on the utmost heights of the sacred mountain [or, the north]. I will ascend above the tops of the clouds; I will make myself like the most High" (Isa. 14:12-14, NIV).

The change in the Ezekiel 28 passage is also pronounced and the language even more developed. It occurs at verse twelve: "This is what the Sovereign Lord says, 'You were in Eden, the garden of God; every precious stone adorned you. . . . Your settings and mountings were made of gold; on the day you were created they were prepared. You were anointed as a guardian cherub [Hebrew, the anointed cherub that covers, or protects], for so I ordained you. You were on the holy mount of God; you walked among the fiery stones. You were blameless in your ways from the day you were created till wickedness was found in you'" (Ezek. 28:12-15, NIV). Something of the previous human king emphasis reasserts itself in verse 16: " 'Through your widespread trade you were filled with violence, and you sinned'" (NIV). But the exalted vision lingers a bit longer: " 'So I drove you in disgrace from the mount of God, and I expelled you, O guardian cherub, from among the fiery stones. Your heart became proud on account of your beauty, and you corrupted your wisdom because of your splendor. So I threw you to the earth'" (16, 17, NIV).

The description here of "the guardian cherub," of his early perfection and blamelessness, his presence in the garden of God, the holy mount, walking among the stones of fire, are items totally irrelevant to the human king of Tyre. There is a strong supposition that here the prophetic vision combines the characteristics of the king of Tyre with those of an evil being in whose spirit he operated, and in so doing reveals something of the history of that evil angel.

The New Testament speaks of angels whom "God did not spare . . . when they sinned" (2 Pet. 2:4, NASB), angels who "did not keep their own domain, but abandoned their proper abode" (Jude 6, NASB). These texts are nonsymbolic counterparts to the Old Testament prophecies.

The very high order of being that is seen behind the kings of Babylon and Tyre disposes us to identify him as the devil himself. If this is true, we have in these two prophecies unique light on the background, original character, and position of Satan, and on the nature of his original fall.

He is seen as a created being, a high order of angel, the light-bearer, guardian of the very presence of God, perfect in beauty and splendor. His downfall involved pride, the corruption of his wisdom, and most significantly, his aspiration to assume the prerogatives of God. Here is the actual starting-point of sinful rebellion and independency in God's universe.

While the early record of Genesis 3 does not identify the "serpent" as Satan, the New Testament does, calling him "that ancient serpent . . . the devil or Satan" (Rev. 12:9, NIV). From the beginning of human history, his design was to bring about a reduplication in the human sphere of his own rebellion and independency. And since Satan's aspiration is to "be like the most High," that is, to usurp the prerogatives of God, we would suspect him of attempting to gain a god-like control over the human race for his own purposes! This was something he could not achieve as long as man remained in fellowship with the true God. His appeal to Eve was true to his real character: "Rebel! Throw off God's yoke! He is not treating you with integrity! Become independent, and you will be like gods. You will find this freedom very good for you." We suspect, from long hindsight, that what he really meant was, "This will be very good for *me*," and that behind all his approach was an insanely destructive malice against God and His creation.

In spite of this success and the evident attitude of hostility and accusation that Satan displays toward mankind—as seen, for example, in his actions against Job and the high priest Joshua—the really outstanding contribution the Old Testament makes on the subject of Satan is its testimony to the absolute sovereignty of God. God rules over Satan and the whole realm of evil.

In the arena of evil, it is as Joseph said to his brothers: "You meant evil against me, but God meant it for good" (Gen. 50:20, NASB). The evil spirit that afflicted King Saul was described as "an evil spirit from the Lord" (1 Sam. 16:14, NIV). The prophet Micaiah described a scene where the Lord was on His throne with all the host of heaven standing around Him discussing the question of how to get King Ahab to attack Ramoth Gilead and die in this battle! A particular spirit (the Hebrew has "*the* spirit") stepped forward and offered to be a spirit of falsehood in the mouth of Ahab's prophets.

Then God said, "You will succeed in luring him. Go and do it" (1 Kings 22:19-22, NIV). The Book of Job records how Satan came before God to try to influence Him: "Stretch out your hand and strike everything he has." God's answer was, "Very well, then, everything he has is in your hands, but on the man himself do not lay a finger" (Job 1:11, 12, NIV). The adversary acknowledged that only by the stretching out of the sovereign hand of God could calamity be brought on Job's possessions. God, on the other hand, used the hand of the adversary to accomplish this disaster, at the same time restricting him from any operation against Job's own person. In all these references the sovereign use that God makes of evil beings is in clear view.

We have referred already to the description in 1 Chronicles of King David's sin in numbering Israel. This is the wording: "Satan rose up against Israel and incited David to take a census of Israel" (1 Chron. 21:1, NIV). It is most startling to discover that in 2 Samuel, written more than five hundred years earlier, the same incident was recorded in these words, "The anger of the Lord burned against Israel, and he incited David against them, saying, Go and count Israel and Judah" (2 Sam. 24:1). This is not a discrepancy at all. It simply reflects the fact that at the earlier period the Old Testament revelation had not yet begun to expose Satan as "the adversary," and all things were attributed to the sovereign action of God, who ruled in all realms. Later the progress of revelation could show how He used Satan to accomplish His purposes.

There is perhaps reason to ask why God would design to bring His innocent creation into contact with an evil being like Satan in Eden. And this, of course, was only the beginning of satanic opposition to the human race. If God is truly sovereign and actually uses the devil to accomplish His own purposes, what are those purposes? How does He design to use Satan's attacks on human beings? God's approach in Eden seems reasonably clear. Adam and Eve had been given a position at the head of the human race by which they were to act for the race at a time of probation and testing. The crucial point would be to determine whether or not they would continue in the state of voluntary fellowship with God for which they had been designed. To make the testing complete, God brought man in touch with the very spirit of rebellion and independency, Satan himself. God's purpose was good; His design was good, even while Satan's purpose was evil. God was functioning with love, Satan with hate. God's sovereignty would be shown even though Satan apparently won a great victory, for redemptive grace would eventually prevail and abound, as would also God's judgment on sin.

The New Testament establishes and enhances all that the Old Testament revelation had introduced with regard to Satan. *Satan* is used uniformly in the New Testament as the official proper name for the devil (some thirty-six times). Many other names are given to him, illustrative of various characteristics and functions of the devil. The idea of "world-rulers of this . . . darkness" (Eph. 6:12, RSV) matches Daniel's picture of evil princes behind the nations. Satan's organized kingdom is displayed much more fully; a full demonic realm under the tight control of Satan is in view (Mark 3:24-26).

Illustrative of the sovereign control of God over Satan's actions, an echo of the Job story is heard in Christ's words to Peter: "Simon, Simon, behold, Satan demanded to have you [lit., asked for you], that he might sift you like wheat, but I have prayed for you that your faith may not fail" (Luke 22:31, RSV). The tense of both main verbs here indicates a specific occasion both for Satan's asking and for Christ's praying. Whatever hatred Satan had for the disciples, he still had to seek permission to shake their faith. The implication is that for God's own purposes He allowed this to happen, but again with a limitation on what he could do, secured by Christ's intercession.

In this account, God's love and redemptive purposes can be seen over against Satan's antagonism. In 2 Thessalonians there is a passage, however, which shows God's sovereign purpose in using Satan against unbelievers in order to bring about their judgment: "The coming of the lawless one will be in accordance with the work of *Satan* displayed in all kinds of counterfeit miracles, signs and wonders, and in every sort of evil that deceives those who are perishing. They perish because they refused to love the truth and so be saved. For this reason *God* sends them a powerful delusion so that they will believe the lie and so that all will be condemned who have not believed the truth but have delighted in wickedness" (2 Thess. 2:9-12, NIV, italics added). This reminds us of God's use of the "spirit of falsehood" to send wicked Ahab to his destruction.

The Bible makes it plain that we do not live in a dualistic universe, where there is a God of good and a god of evil—two equal and opposite kingdoms in a see-saw conflict. There is one God only, even though there is indeed a high-ranking creature who epitomizes rebellion and the spirit of independency, and who seeks with malice to usurp God's prerogatives and lord it over God's creation.

The New Testament follows through on the extent to which Satan was allowed to succeed in his attempt to exercise control over the human race through man's fall into rebellion. Several passages fill in the picture. In his first epistle John says, "He who does what is sinful is of the devil, because the devil has been sinning from the beginning" (1 John 3:8, NIV). Then there are Christ's words to His enemies, "You belong to your father, the devil, and you want to carry out your father's desire" (John 8:44, NIV). By all means the most unmistakable description and devastating indictment is that of Paul in Ephesians 2: "Time was when you were dead in your sins and wickedness, when you followed the evil ways of this present age, when you obeyed the commander of the spiritual powers of the air, the spirit now at work among God's rebel subjects" (Eph. 2:1, 2, NEB). It is alarmingly clear that Satan now operates easily in sinful mankind through the very rebellion and independency that he himself originally encouraged.

All of this leads us to understand that for a Christian, too, Satan is a real foe and a formidable opponent to a walk of fellowship with God. The changes that come about in our situation when we are converted to faith in Christ do not remove us from the scene in which Satan "prowls around like a roaring lion looking for someone to devour" (1 Pet. 5:8, NIV). Nor has the "rebel streak" discussed in the preceding chapter been removed from us. Therefore Christians are instructed in the New Testament to "submit yourselves, then, to God. Resist the devil and he will flee from you" (James 4:7, NIV). This teaches us that our independency must be dealt with before we can expect the devil to heed our resistance. Or to say it another way: independency, even in Christians, will permit Satan to wield some measure of influence over them.

So it is Christians who are warned not to "give the devil a foothold" (Eph. 4:27, NIV); not to be "unaware of his schemes!" (2 Cor. 2:11, NIV); and in three different locations "to resist" him (Eph. 6:13; James 4:7; 1 Peter 5:9).

Much more instruction may be found in the New Testament concerning Satan's devices and activities. Our present concern, however, has been to see him as the original and continuing aggravator of human independency, the arch rebel himself, who seeks to be the prevailing spirit in human affairs.

Those of us who would learn to walk in fellowship with God would do well to heed both the reality of God's sovereign control over the realm of evil and the vulnerability that our sinful rebellion creates with respect to the devil. Dating back to the very beginning of human history there has been an affinity between our rebel spirit and *the* rebel spirit who began the war with God. Both must be dealt with, if we are to have real freedom and intimacy with God.

SIX

The World

Human beings were designed by their Maker to be social creatures. Their best interests are served and God's glory displayed when they interact with others. Their ability to relate to one another grew out of their capacity to interact with God; their loss of fellowship with God deeply blighted social life as well. This blighted social interaction, magnified and compounded by centuries of ungodliness and satanic activity, has resulted in the complex and evil world in which we live. As redemption restores to us the potential of walking with God, the surrounding world becomes a severe obstacle to that walk.

Put this in terms of love. The two great standards for man are: love God and love each other. These loves interact with each other. If we do not love God, we will not love each other; if we do not love each other, we will not easily love God, in whose image we are made.

To be involved daily in a society where neither kind of love prevails is to encounter pressure against both.

There is still enormous potential for mutual accomplishments in this world. Even though the curse of sin pervades man's joint endeavors, the capacity to join hands in the sharing of knowledge, natural gifts, creativity, the development of natural resources, and scores of other functions, is still much in evidence. Man is sinful, indeed, but he is still a social creature irresistibly drawn into mutual endeavors.

Magnificent testimonials to this potential exist. Whenever we ponder the integration of human efforts and wisdom that goes into the construction of a skyscraper or a mile-long bridge—the skills of designers, implementers, and coordinators, along with the sheer beauty of the product—we have to be impressed. The same may be said about a transportation system, a communications network, a symphony played by a great orchestra, an intricate financial system, or an entertaining movie. As human beings we rightly find such achievements highly pleasing.

Yet Scripture warns us that this world system is a great hazard to a walk with God. "Do not love the world, nor the things in the world. If anyone loves the world, the love of the Father is not in him" (1 John 2:15, NASB). Why is this so?

The primary pressure we encounter in the world is its *ungodliness*. If ungodliness is defined as lack of reverential awareness of God in the functions of life, this surely describes the world scene. "The world through its wisdom did not come to know God," said Paul to the Corinthians (1 Cor. 1:21, NASB). Whether we are reading *Time* magazine or *Newsweek* or *Popular Mechanics*, the outlook will be almost uniformly godless. It will be equally true of a tome on nuclear physics or the *Field Guide to Birds*. The thinking of this world does not center around the knowledge of God. The great systems of thought and culture do not know Him, whether they involve philosophies of education, Madison Avenue advertising know-how, or television and entertainment. It is as though the Originator, Sustainer, and Controller of this universe did not exist!

The problem of ungodliness in this world system is aggravated by the fact that human beings are still incurably religious. If worship is respect and reverence paid to *worth*, then much worship takes place in this world. Mankind continually erects value structures and shows a strong need to assign something as the top or center of them. This ultimate good becomes the central value of their world, the value that gives meaning to all the rest of life. It becomes their god, and they give themselves to it. Every system of thought or culture pattern in this world is oriented toward the worship of some god. The Christian is not only confronted constantly by the absence of true godliness in this world, but is bombarded by substitute gods—false worship.

The passage quoted a moment ago from 1 John 2 goes on to speak of the world in these terms: "For all that is in the world, the lust of the flesh and the lust of the eyes and the boastful pride of life, is not from the

Father, but is from the world" (1 John 2:16, NASB). The world is characterized by the "desire of the flesh." The problem that a Christian encounters in his own nature, that of natural independency and rebellion, is a multiplied reality in the world around him.

It may seem strange that the human inclination to be autonomous and self-seeking should exist side by side with the human inclination to be social and to interact with other human beings. Yet anyone who has tried to climb the company ladder to success knows that it is all too true. "Looking out for number one" is both a private and a public creed. The advertising world subtly or blatantly tells us that we owe it to ourselves to satisfy every craving, pamper every desire, and get what we want. No price is too great to pay for that! In the absence of the fear of God, flesh runs rampant in this world.

This world is much more than merely a place where a lot of individuals spar for their rights. Because of their social capacity, and the necessity laid on them to function together in many ways, human beings develop an interlocking network of godless desires. One of the fascinating accounts of the Bible is the story of the Tower of Babel and the separating of the human family by the confusion of tongues. The cooperative project that men had undertaken was not one that God approved, and in order to diminish their capacity to go on corporate ego trips of this sort, God scattered them by creating different languages. What this would eventually mean in terms of national, ethnic, and linguistic pecu-

liarities, balances of power, wars, and partisan loyalties
is startling to contemplate. Because of sin, the unity
and social capacity that had been built into man was
now too dangerous to be tolerated in any total form. It
would result in too much collaboration in evil (cf. Gen.
11:5-9).

Since mankind does operate in groupings, the desires
of the flesh—the jealous promotion of personal
rights—escalates to the corporate level. Doing what *I*
want is enlarged to doing what *we* want. Families strive
to defend their rights against other families; political
units clash with other units in a struggle for rights;
industrial concerns wield all the power they can for
their own advantage; nations foster a loyalty that says,
"My country right or wrong" in pushing for "the national interest." For pride and glory, social groupings go on
ego trips just as the individuals who belong to them do.
Not only is extensive pressure to conform brought to
bear on members of these groups, but the individuals'
nature readily and naturally responds to it.

Power becomes tremendously important in the world
system. Money, political know-how or connections,
skillful propaganda, the exploitation of fears and human
longings, threats, and rewards are used shamelessly to
secure the desired ends—and all without the fear of
God.

Behind this scene of an essentially godless and fleshly
world lies the reality of satanic dominion over it. The
Bible says bluntly, "The whole world is under the control of the evil one" (1 John 5:19, NIV). Satan made this

claim for himself in his temptation of Christ: "The devil led him up to a high place and showed him in an instant all the kingdoms of the world. And he said to him, 'I will give you all their authority and splendor, for it has been given to me, and I can give it to anyone I want to' " (Luke 4:5, 6, NIV).

The mere fact that man's flesh provides Satan operating room and some measure of functional control of human life opens a large door for the devil's operation in this world. This connection is clear from the association of phrases in Ephesians 2:2: "You formerly walked according to the course of this world, according to the prince of the power of the air" (NASB). The scriptural emphasis on the sovereignty of God with respect to Satan and the way God uses him for the ultimate accomplishment of divine purposes lends weight to Satan's claim that his position in this world has been "given" to him.

The hatred of the world for Christ and His followers (John 15:18, 19) and the tribulation that the body of Christ is promised in this world reflect Satan's own animosity. So also does the sheer force that temptation sometimes assumes. The deceptions of this world betray the authorship of the deceiver, and indeed false doctrine is described in the Bible as teaching promoted by deceiving spirits (1 Tim. 4:1, NIV).

In addition, the emphasis in both Old and New Testaments on the way organized powers of the satanic kingdom stand behind world rulers and nations becomes important to our understanding of this world. The tides and trends of evil in the world system suggest a mastermind behind them, even while the Lord God continues to be sovereign over all.

In order to see clearly the conflict caused by our position as Christians in the world, we need to ponder the nature of the Christian community. God purposed a human society in which He was to be known, loved, and honored, in which love would be expressed, gifts and capacities harmonized to the glory of God, and in which encouragement, caring, and burden-bearing would be realities. This design is now focused primarily in the new humanity of Christ's body. Christians are those whom God has rescued "from the dominion of darkness" and brought into "the kingdom of the Son he loves" (Col. 1:13, NIV). We are to be "blameless and innocent, children of God above reproach in the midst of a crooked and perverse generation, among whom you appear as lights in the world" (Phil. 2:15, NASB).

It is in this world, with its ungodly, fleshly, and satanic characteristics, that God has planted, like an oasis surrounded by desert, His new order, His new humanity. He has great plans for the social life and interactions of His redeemed people. This becomes apparent when we reflect on the sheer volume of material in the New Testament that deals with relationships of Christians. Successful demonstration of redeemed human characteristics is a major part of the Christian witness in the world. Christ prays for His own to this end: "I have sent them into the world. . . . I have given them the glory that you gave me, that they may be one as we are one:

I in them and you in me. May they be brought to complete unity to let the world know that you sent me and have loved them . . ." (John 17:18, 22, 23, NIV). We also remember His statement, "All men will know that you are my disciples if you love one another" (John 13:35, NIV).

The marvel is that such a plan should involve people who, though brought to Christ, are still cut out of the same piece of cloth as the rest of humanity, still inclined to rebellion, vulnerable to the enemy's attacks. The world presses in on them from every side. Many of its value structures and ungodly ways tend constantly to infiltrate the Church. We have to be warned vigorously by Scripture not to be pushed into the world's mold (Rom. 12:2), to be in the world but not of it (John 17:15, 16), to use the things of the world but not be engrossed in them (1 Cor. 7:31, NIV), not to heed the demon voices of false teaching (1 John 4:1-3), not to worship the god of money (Matt. 6:24).

Perhaps this sounds overwhelming. But Scripture is not pessimistic at all. "In this world you will have trouble," said our Lord. "But take heart! I have overcome the world" (John 16:33, NIV). We are commissioned to be agents of Christ's worldwide evangelistic program, to bring the good news to all people, and to demonstrate its effectiveness (Matt. 28:18-20; John 16:7-11).

Not only are we to be recruiting agents for the new humanity, but we are instructed to be "the salt of the earth" in the old (Matt. 5:13). Keeping ourselves "unstained by the world" (James 1:27, NASB), we are to find the balance of being those who are drawing people constantly into the new kingdom and at the same time those who have a cultural mandate to influence redemptively the old order.

And so we live in this present evil world. We have to use it; we have to work in it; we must find ways to enjoy recreation in it. Its currency is in our pockets and bank accounts; its markets service our daily needs. Its woes call for our sympathies, its structures for our prayers. It is attractive and deadly. It is ungodly, fleshly, and devilish. It gathers up all the opposition to a walk with God and throws it at us from every side. Yet it affords us the great stage for our Christian drama: for demonstrating the victory of Jesus Christ and calling people to a new world in which dwells righteousness.

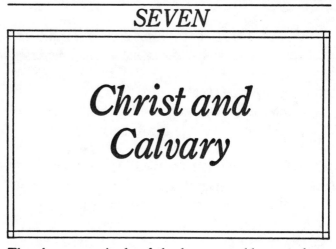

SEVEN

Christ and Calvary

The sheer magnitude of the human problem can have two very different effects on our thinking. It can serve either to make us cynical and pessimistic about our possibilities as Christians, or it can serve to awaken us to the surpassing greatness of Christ's redemptive work. A great sickness calls for a great physician. The fact of the matter is that the more we look at the gospel, the more astoundingly *good* the "good news" about Jesus Christ is.

The Apostle Paul told the Corinthians that the gospel of Christ had two great focal points: that He "died for our sins according to the Scriptures," and that He "was raised on the third day according to the Scriptures" (1 Cor. 15:3, 4, NIV). As soon as Peter expressed his great confession of faith in Christ as his Messiah, Jesus began for the first time to tell his disciples that "he must go to Jerusalem . . . be killed and on the third day be raised to life" (Matt. 16:21, NIV). But Peter resisted this knowledge, as did all the disciples, until the very day he saw Jesus die. After the resurrection, Jesus gave all the disciples an extensive Bible study from the Old Testament centering on this dual truth: "This is what I told you while I was still with you. . . . Then he opened their minds so they could understand the Scriptures. . . . This is what is written: The Christ will suffer and rise from the dead on the third day" (Luke 24:44, 45, NIV). Peter's sermon at Pentecost clearly reflected the impact of this new understanding of Scripture, and Paul's statement to the Corinthians still reflected it. It had become the settled awareness of the Church that its message of good news centered around these two great facts. For all who would grasp the dynamics of godliness, this is where the good news is, too, and this will be the subject matter of the next two chapters of our study.

To understand Christ's redemptive acts we must first grasp the *capacity* in which He acted. One of the more startling ways in which the New Testament describes this is to call Him "the second man," "the last Adam" (1 Cor. 15:45, 47). The most complete statement of the idea behind these terms is the last part of Romans 5. There Paul tells of the unique capacity given to Adam and to Christ to represent the human race in the things they did. The fact that 1 Corinthians 15 calls Christ the *second* man and the *last* Adam, indicates that Adam and Christ were the only two persons who would ever have this capacity.

Adam *was* the human race when he was tested in the

Garden and fell into sin. What happened to him was happening to the rest of mankind in him. Within the sphere of his life the experience of sin and death came, afterward becoming the condition of all who followed him into this world.

Once more, much later in time, it was given to one Man to occupy the same kind of relationship to humankind. Miraculously preserved at birth from receiving the inheritance of sin from His forebears, He was given the capacity to stand again for all mankind and to affect them by what He did. Once more the race is tested in one Man, and the outcome is shared by all who follow in His family. This is Jesus Christ, the last Adam.

Somehow, to say that Jesus was our great Representative or even our Substitute is to say too little. We shall see that a number of Scripture's shades of meaning imply something more. Somehow it was true that He was so identified with humanity that He *was* the human race in what He did. It became possible for the whole human problem to be gathered into this one Person and there be dealt with, not just representatively or symbolically, but really and totally. Results were achieved within the sphere of His own Person, which may properly be said to have happened to humanity in Him. Christ became the sphere within which God handled the human problem.

This capacity comes most clearly into view at Calvary. But before that is studied, we must see the road He walked to get there. It was the road of fellowship with His Father and perfect obedience. This is in stark contrast with the failure of the first Adam to remain in fellowship with God, and in contrast with his choice of rebellion.

There is a tiny but profound biography of Christ in Philippians 2. In the midst of it occurs this statement: "And being found in human form he humbled himself and became obedient unto death" (Phil. 2:8, RSV). What we sometimes underemphasize is that this was not just a final great act of obedience at Calvary, but a lifetime of total obedience to His Father.

The Philippians statement makes plain that obedience is the characteristic which ought to go along with being human. When Jesus took human form, He laid aside the independent exercise of His divine prerogatives and "learned" obedience, as Hebrews 5:8 says. All the while that He lived here, He was living as man ought to live: in full fellowship with the Father and absolutely fulfilling His will. This relationship was clearly important to Him, and it is quite startling to observe how often He spoke of it: "I tell you the truth, the Son can do nothing by himself; he can only do what he sees his Father doing. . . . By myself I can do nothing; I judge only as I hear, and my judgment is just, for I seek not to please myself but him who sent me. . . . My teaching is not my own. It comes from him who sent me. . . . I do nothing on my own, but speak just what the Father has taught me. . . . The one who sent me is with me; he has not left me alone, for I do always what pleases him. . . . The Father who sent me commanded me what to say and how to say it . . . whatever I say is just what the Father told me to say" (John 5:19, 30; 7:16; 8:28, 29; 12:49, 50, NIV).

That the cross was the place where this path of obedience was leading was plain in Jesus' mind. It gave Him much anguish. We hear Him on one occasion unexpectedly say, "Now my heart is troubled [the Greek verb indicates a deep state of agitation], and what shall I say? 'Father, save me from this hour?' No, it was for this very reason I came to this hour. Father, glorify your name!" (John 12:27, 28, NIV). The same agitation came to its peak in the Garden of Gethsemane, when Jesus prays "with loud cries and tears," "Father, if you are willing, take this cup from me; yet not my will but yours be done" (Luke 22:42, NIV). He learned obedience by the things he suffered.

All this active obeying was done by Jesus in His capacity as man; indeed, in His capacity as *the* Man. He was obeying for humanity; He was walking in constant fellowship with His Father—the reverse of the first Adam's failure. He was doing this for us. Do we have trouble saying, "Not my will but yours be done"? The first thing that the last Adam provides for us in His personal experience is a life of perfect obedience and fellowship, done in our behalf.

Consider His voluntary reversal of personal roles. One whose eternal right was to be Master became the consummate Servant. This adds clarity to our understanding of what Satan was attempting to do when he tempted Christ in the wilderness. His repeated approach to Jesus was, "If you are the *Son of God*, then do this or that." But the things he was suggesting were no part of the works the Father had for the Son to do while He was here. The devil sought to have Him abandon His role of obedience and revert to His God-right of independent initiative. Although the setting and background were quite different, for both Adams the devil's attack was the same: to make independency attractive. Adam fell, and we with him; Christ obeyed, and we with Him!

The cross was the climax of Christ's obedience. But now it becomes something more and different from His active compliance with the will of the Father. Jesus faced not only the goal of starting mankind over again on the right foot, so to speak, but also of dealing with the consequences of the fall. In a great act of passive obedience, He allowed the weight of evil to be placed on Himself at Calvary and there to be judged. "God made him who had no sin to be sin for us" (2 Cor. 5:21, NIV).

Early in His public ministry Jesus used a striking image from the Old Testament to describe this reality of His cross: "Just as Moses lifted up the snake in the desert, so the Son of man must be lifted up, that everyone who believes in him may have eternal life" (John 3:14, 15, NIV). "Lamb of God who takes away the sin of the world" or "suffering servant" we can tolerate as images, but "snake on a pole in the desert" seems so gross as to be unthinkable. It is no more gross, however, than the statement that "God made him *to be sin* for us." In the snake symbol we see the gathering up of all human rebellion and sin in the Person of the suffering Christ. We even see in the shadows the serpent of Eden, the very spirit of rebellion and godlessness. All this came down with excruciating pain on the spotless soul of One who had never had a word or a thought out of harmony with His Father. And with this miraculously awful reality came the wrath and judgment of His Father and a totally hellish loss of fellowship with Him.

"It was the Lord's will to crush him and cause him to suffer . . . the Lord makes his life a guilt offering. . . . Surely he took up our infirmities and carried our sorrows, yet we considered him stricken by God, smitten by him and afflicted. But he was pierced for our transgressions, he was crushed for our iniquities; the punishment that brought us peace was upon him. . . . We all, like sheep, have gone astray, each of us has turned to his own way; and the Lord has laid on him the iniquity of us all. . . . He poured out his life unto death" (Isa. 53:4-6, 12, NIV).

The great agony of all human history was voiced in Jesus' cry on Calvary, "My God, my God, why hast thou forsaken me?" Heaven's fellowship, the very intimacy of the Trinity, was broken at Calvary, in order that our fellowship with God might be restored. Jesus' conquest of sin was effective and complete. "Now he has appeared once for all at the end of the ages to do away with sin by the sacrifice of himself" (Heb. 9:26, NIV). Fully encompassing the problem in His own Person, He fully solves it and ends it by taking it down into death with Himself.

Jesus at Calvary was also dealing with the satanic forces that had infiltrated and dominated the human scene. We catch a glimpse of what was about to happen in Christ's words in Gethsemane to the band of arresting agents, "This is your hour, and the power [authority] of darkness" (Luke 22:53, RSV). Up to this point, Christ had resisted, outwitted, and totally dominated Satan and his hosts at every turn. Now Satan was given free rein to work his worst. It was logical that this should be. If sin is what gives place to the devil in human lives, then when *the* Man was made sin, it might be expected that Satan would be allowed to bring his full power to bear on Him.

In His dying, Jesus also was completely effective in overcoming Satan. The writer of Hebrews put it strongly. "He . . . shared in their humanity so that by his death he might destroy him who holds the power of death—that is, the devil" (Heb. 2:14, NIV).

There is one translation of Colossians 2 which, if correct, adds dramatic significance to statements of Christ's victory over the satanic kingdom. In verse 15 the NIV reads: "And having *disarmed* the powers and authorities, he made a public spectacle of them, triumphing over them by the cross" (italics added). A reflexive translation of the verb is equally possible, so that it would read, "he threw off from himself [like a garment] the powers and authorities." All agree that the same verb in precisely the same form is used reflexively in the following chapter, where Christians are spoken of as having "put off *from themselves* the old man with his deeds" (3:9, KJV). There is good reason for translating it this way also in 2:15. Jesus Christ at Calvary, as the last Adam and the originator of a new race and a new humanity, threw off from Himself, in a final and total way, the clinging garment of satanic oppression which He had allowed to envelop Him. As He went down into death, He escaped Satan's clutches forever—indeed, brought Satan down with Him. This all happened within the sphere of Christ's own Person and experience.

So it is also with the human experience of death, especially that spiritual death which is alienation from the life of God. Christ had been "made for a little while lower than the angels [that is, human] . . . that by the grace of God he might taste death for every one" (Heb. 2:9, NASB). As the Puritans delighted to say, His death was the death of death: He "abolished death, and brought life and immortality to light through the gospel" (2 Tim. 1:10, NASB).

Stressing the fact that these accomplishments were worked out completely within the sphere of Jesus' Person and experience gives us an understanding of some unique and powerful statements of Scripture. Romans 4:25 is one. The *New American Standard Bible* is grammatically correct in giving what might be considered a difficult reading here: "He . . . was delivered up *because of* our transgressions, and was raised *because of* our justification" (italics added). If this is true, what is this text saying? That Jesus became the sphere in which our sins were punished is clear enough: He indeed died "because of" our transgressions. But as He does so, He also receives in His own Person and experience the full judicial acquittal for us (justification). His resurrection took place *because* we had been justified in His Person. Nowhere else in Scripture is there a hint that His resurrection caused our justification; rather, His resurrection was caused, at least in part, by our justification! All of our salvation is worked out in His Person and experience. There it happened and there the results reside. Salvation is truly in Jesus Christ.

A similar statement is made in 1 Peter 1:3: "In his great mercy he has given us new birth into a living hope through the resurrection of Jesus Christ from the dead" (NIV). Since this is on the resurrection side of Jesus' work, we will come back to it in the next chapter. For now the point is the outlook of these Scriptures: that these great things we need—justification and new birth—were accomplished for us, and in a sense happened to us, in the Person and work of Christ.

One of the consequences of this fact is the realization that we cannot merit nor earn our salvation, nor can we find it anywhere else but in Jesus Christ. Our contact with its benefits comes entirely from our contact with Him.

Our faith in Jesus Christ is the vital point at which a magnificent process breaks into our lives—a process which "began" in eternity in the mind of God: "He chose us in him before the foundation of the world, that we should be holy and blameless in his sight" (Eph. 1:4, NASB). It continued in the mind of Christ at Calvary:

"who loved *me* and gave himself for *me*" (Gal. 2:20, NIV, italics added). I, too, along with Paul, was in His mind at Calvary! God had so invested Him with the power to atone for my sins and deal with my problems that just as soon as He died, I was justified! Just as soon as He came out of the grave, I was born of God! It would be 2,000 years before my earthly existence would even begin, but it was all accomplished in Jesus then and there. It came into my life when I believed. I could not earn it; I could not deserve it; I could only accept Him and it by faith!

In Jesus Christ, then, is not only the full basis for forgiveness and justification, but also for restoration to fellowship with God. Our reconciliation has already been accomplished in Christ: "The death he died, he died to sin once for all; but the life he lives, he lives to God" (Rom. 6:10, NIV). "God was reconciling the world to himself in Christ, not counting men's sins against them" (2 Cor. 5:19, NIV).

One of the great redemption passages of the New Testament is Ephesians 2:11-22. What makes it unusual and pertinent to any study of the cross is the fact that it deals with troubled human relationships, the loss of fellowship among people.

The particular relationship discussed here is the Jew-Gentile division. Through much of human history this has stood as a prime example of irreconcilable animosity. Gentiles are spoken of by Paul in this passage as "excluded" and "foreigners" in verse 12; as "far away" in verse 13. Verse 14 speaks of the "barrier, the dividing wall of hostility"; and verse 16 mentions hostility again.

Whatever this situation involved in terms of the fleshly drive toward pride, self-protection, and self-aggrandizement, it also had deep cultural, historical, and racial undertones. It was a psychologically complex situation.

But here again the emphasis is on what Christ accomplished in His own Person. Verse 13: "In Christ Jesus you who once were far away have been brought near through the blood of Christ." The death of Jesus Christ at Calvary was the solution to the problem of human separation. Somehow, Christ identified Himself with this dimension of sin, too, so that it could be dealt with in His own Person.

This is stated even more strongly in verse 16, where the NIV has the words, "to reconcile both of them to God through the cross, by which he put to death their hostility." For this passage to speak of Jew-Gentile hostility as being slain in the death of Jesus Christ implies a tremendous scope to His accomplishment there. There is a dimension of world order, of racial and cultural history, in the death of that unique Man at Calvary. Here is the foundation for correcting the disorders which fall under the second table of the law, those which violate the love of neighbor.

There is some sense in which Jesus Christ gathered together in Himself the entire world with all of its problems for which He was the atonement. When He died He brought that old order into death in its entirety. As our Lord approached the cross, He said, "Now is the time for judgment on this world; now the prince of this world will be driven out" (John 12:31, NIV). There is a large hint of this also in Paul's statement in Galatians 6:14: "May I never boast except in the cross of our Lord Jesus Christ, through which the world has been crucified to me, and I to the world" (NIV). The Pandora's box which had been opened by the first Adam's rebellion was closed and destroyed by the last Adam. As far as His Person is concerned, the old order has passed away. Only the new exists.

All these things have been worked out in the last Adam. Apart from Him there is no way that we can pay for our sins, find renewed fellowship with God, overcome the devil, or love our neighbor. What we need is to come into living touch with Jesus Christ, where all these things have been secured. We need to be part of the new race of which He is the living Head, the One in whom our salvation is complete.

EIGHT

Christ Alive

The second great focus of the gospel is the resurrection of Jesus Christ. Scripture speaks of our being saved by Christ's death; it also speaks of our being saved by His life (Rom. 5:10).

At the point of death Jesus cried, "It is finished." This had a large reference: the great work of atonement was done. Mankind's ills had been engulfed by Christ and conquered. But much of the redemptive sequence was yet ahead. The full consequences of His death were yet to be received in His Person and experience. He was not at all finished acting in His capacity as the last Adam, the representative man. There is great significance for us in the chain of events which starts with the empty tomb and continues to this very moment. Christianity does not present us with a memory only; it presents us with the living Christ—active, powerful, glorious.

The resurrection of Jesus Christ is the obviously

unique miracle of human history. He did what no man before or since has done—He came out of the grave on the other side of death! Others have been raised from the dead; indeed, Lazarus spent a longer time in the tomb than Jesus did! But he came out of the grave still mortal, only to die again. Christ came out of the grave *immortal,* totally triumphant over death. Death, so far as His Person was concerned, was permanently put away. "We know that since Christ was raised from the dead, he cannot die again; death no longer has mastery over him" (Rom. 6:9, NIV).

It is clear that this was Jesus' unique personal experience. While there is a sense in which we share the results of what he did, the physical experience of death and resurrection is still ahead for us, whereas it has been completed for Him. He is the one totally free man. In terms of His own Person, our sin which He had embraced has been irrevocably put away; our death is totally abolished; our adversary thoroughly and finally defeated, and this evil world brought to an end. The Person of Jesus Christ is free from the miseries of the race. While we for whom He accomplished these things still live in the sphere where they operate, He does not—except by His Spirit and in His people. Where He lives, only righteousness, godliness, holiness, beauty, and power exist.

At the resurrection Jesus was not only free from our human ills, but He also was the beginning of a new humanity, a new creation. This was dramatically and immediately demonstrated by the fact that He came out of the grave with a new resurrection body. For forty unique days His disciples had the unparalleled experience of observing the first and only example of such a body! Jesus went to some lengths to demonstrate to them that it was a real body—that He was not a ghost. Also they touched Him; Mary Magdalene perhaps hugged Him (a very acceptable translation of John 20:17 is "Stop clinging to me"—Arndt and Gingrich, *Lexicon*, p. 102); He ate in their presence, and He said directly, "A ghost does not have flesh and bones, as you see I have" (Luke 24:39, NIV).

There were strange things about that body, however. His followers saw Him only about a dozen times in forty days. We have not the faintest clue where He was between these appearances. He had the disconcerting ability to appear and disappear in their presence. Mark 16:12 says that "Jesus appeared in a different form to two of them while they were walking in the country" (NIV). The Luke account of this story says that "they were kept from recognizing Him" (Luke 24:16, NIV). Yet Jesus took pains to show them the marks of His crucifixion (John 20:25, 27). So there was continuity between the old body and the new.

Then came the day when a large number of them saw Him "taken up before their very eyes, and a cloud hid him from their sight" (Acts 1:9, NIV). Angelic messengers appeared to them and said, "This same Jesus, who has been taken from you into heaven, will come back in the same way you have seen him go into heaven" (Acts 1:11, NIV). A startling implication of this statement is the possibility that Jesus Christ, since He went away in His resurrection body and will apparently return in it, is right now present somewhere in this universe in that resurrection body, the only completed example of a new humanity!

Two other passages bear this thought out, mind-boggling though it may seem. Paul wrote to the Philippians, "Our citizenship is in heaven. And we eagerly await a Savior from there, the Lord Jesus Christ, who by the power that enables him to bring everything under his control, will transform our lowly bodies so that they will be like his glorious body" (Phil. 3:20, 21, NIV). This is echoed by John: "What we will be has not yet been made known. But we know that when he appears, we shall be like him, for we shall see him *as he is*" (1 John 3:2, NIV). Indeed, "we will all be changed. . . . For the perishable must clothe itself with the imperishable, and the mortal with immortality" (1 Cor. 15:51, 53, NIV).

So far this is true only of the great Forerunner. He is "the firstfruits of those who have fallen asleep" (1 Cor. 15:20, NIV). Look where we will among men (this is the argument of Heb. 2:6-10), we do not see now in the human race the glory God originally intended for humanity. "But we see Jesus . . . now crowned with glory and honor because he suffered death" (Heb. 2:9, NIV). Though He will indeed bring many brethren to glory, at this point He is the only example in fullness of the new humanity. The New Testament expression "new man" is commonly misused, as though it refers to some part of a Christian's personality—a new nature which has become part of his being as a result of conversion. While this touches on some elements of truth, the New Testament use of the expression has a different meaning. Its first usage occurs in Ephesians: "For he himself is our peace, who has made the two one [i.e., Jew and Gentile] and has destroyed the barrier, the dividing wall of hostility. . . . His purpose was to create *in himself* one *new man* out of the two, thus making peace" (Eph. 2:14-16, NIV).

In the ultimate sense, Jesus Christ Himself is the new man. "If anyone is in Christ," as the text then literally says: "*a new creation exists;* the old has gone, and the new has come" (2 Cor. 5:17). A new humanity, a new creation, exists in the risen Christ. It exists only in a derived sense in Christians. So Ephesians 4:24 tells Christians to be "clothed with" or to "put on *the new man,* created in righteousness and holiness of the truth." Romans 13:14, however, gives precisely the same command by saying, "Be clothed with" or "put on the Lord Jesus Christ." Jesus *is* the new man.

At times we may have puzzled over the absoluteness of the expression, "the old has gone, the new has come" (2 Cor. 5:17, NIV). It seems most unrealistic to think this when we are still wrestling bitterly with the old. We have the same problem with other statements: if Christ has done away with sin by the sacrifice of himself, why does Scripture elsewhere tell us to throw off sin (Heb. 12:1, NIV)? If Scripture tells us in one place that Christ destroyed Satan (Heb. 2:14), why does it tell us in another that Satan "prowls around like a roaring lion looking for someone to devour" (1 Pet. 5:8, NIV)? We take a long step toward understanding these apparent discrepancies when we realize that the completeness—the *"done-ness"* of salvation—exists only in the Person and experience of Christ, who alone is on the other side of our human miseries.

When we look at the fact that Christ in a sense *was* the human race when these things were accomplished in Him, we can say with accuracy that "we died and our life is now hidden with Christ in God," and that "we have been raised with Christ" (Col. 3:1, 3). But we can also understand the exhortations that tell us to "put to death" the misdeeds of the body (Rom. 8:13), to "put off the old man" (Eph. 4:22), and to "put on Jesus Christ" (Rom. 13:14). The experiences are His, first, in all perfection. They are ours also in the potential of our relationship with Him. But in our experience they are derived and yet to be completed. So we still "groan inwardly as we wait eagerly for . . . the redemption of our bodies" (Rom. 8:23).

At the same time the eye of faith is fixed on a risen and triumphant Savior, who has in Himself the full fruit of His victory, and who is the beginning of a new humanity and a new creation.

We seldom treat Jesus' ascension as though it were really important. Yet it seemed to be something He personally considered with great anticipation. There is a surprising glimpse of this in something He said to His disciples in the upper room: "You heard me say, 'I am going away and I am coming back to you.' If you loved me, you would be glad that I am going to the Father, for the Father is greater than I" (John 14:28, NIV). There is almost a wistful note to this statement. He does not say, "If you only knew what this would mean eventually to you, or what great things will culminate when I go away, you would be glad." He says, in effect, "If you only knew what this will mean to me, and really cared about me, you would be glad for me that I am going back to the Father. This will be a great event in my life."

And indeed it would be! Hear Him pray a few minutes later: "Father, the time has come. Glorify your Son, that your Son may glorify you. . . . I have brought you glory on earth by completing the work you gave me to do. And now, Father, glorify me in your presence with the glory I had with you before the world began" (John 17:1, 4, 5, NIV). Jesus had "emptied" Himself, humbled Himself, veiled His glory when He came into our scene. Now He prays, "Give me back my glory that I laid aside to become human."

In addition to the brightness and splendor of His unveiled deity, there is the glory Jesus receives in His humanity, the glory that mankind had lost: "We see Jesus . . . now crowned with glory and honor because he suffered death" (Heb. 2:9, NIV). In His humanity as well as His deity He was to be crowned with unspeakable glory. Ahead of Him lay the tremendous estate described in Philippians, because He had been obedient to the death of the cross: "Therefore God exalted Him to the highest place and gave him the name that is above every name, that at the name of Jesus every knee should bow, in heaven and on earth and under the earth, and every tongue confess that Jesus Christ is Lord, to the glory of God the Father" (Phil. 2:9-11, NIV).

How wonderful it is to realize that this has happened to Jesus. Against the backdrop of humiliation and shame on the cross, His present glory and beauty are beyond imagination! When the Apostle John saw Him in glory—that beloved disciple who had been Jesus' closest friend on earth—he fell at His feet as though dead, awestruck, and had to be lifted up gently and reassured by the Lord. Here is the picture of Christ as John saw Him: "Among the lampstands was someone 'like a son of man,' dressed in a robe reaching down to his feet and with a golden sash around his chest. His head and hair were white like wool, and his eyes were like blazing fire. His feet were like bronze glowing in a furnace, and his voice was like the sound of rushing waters. In his right hand he held seven stars, and out of his mouth came a sharp, double-edged sword. His face was like the sun shining in all its brilliance" (Rev. 1:13-16, NIV). Great figurative language, we say! Indeed it is, its only weakness being that no human language can possibly describe the surpassing glory, power, and beauty of the exalted Christ!

Look, ye saints, the sight is glorious!
  See the Man of sorrows now;
From the fight returned victorious,
  Every knee to Him shall bow.
    Crown Him!
    Crown Him!
Crowns become the Victor's brow.

Hark! those bursts of acclamation!
  Hark! those loud triumphant chords!
Jesus takes the highest station;
  Oh what joy the sight affords!
    Crown Him!
    Crown Him!
King of kings, and Lord of lords!

(Thomas Kelly, 1809)

This is our Savior Jesus Christ now! He is real! He is there! We do not worship a memory of One who walked the earth two thousand years ago; we do not merely seek to put into practice certain ideals enunciated by One who no longer has any reality to us. Our Savior lives in great glory. He is our sovereign Head. We serve the living Christ.

How we should sorrow that our eyes of faith are so dim that we do not see Him as He is, that we have ever been ashamed to bear testimony to Him! How we ought to regret that there ever has been a time when we did not fully own His kingship over us, that we ever withheld an ounce of service or debated any claim of His on our lives, our strength, our goods! What shame that we have ever considered any problem too great for Him to handle, or that we have substituted paltry plans of our own contrivance for His sovereign use of our lives! How we should sorrow for the times when we have taken glory to ourselves that belonged to Him!

The writer of Hebrews presents a vivid and somewhat startling picture of the present priesthood of Christ: "Now there were many of those priests, since death prevented them from continuing in office; but because Jesus lives forever, he has a permanent priesthood. Therefore he is able to save completely those who come to God through him because he always lives to intercede for them" (Heb. 7:23-25, NIV). "The point of what we are saying is this: We do have such a high priest, who sat down at the right hand of the throne of the Majesty in heaven, and who serves in the sanctuary, the true tabernacle set up by the Lord, not by man" (Heb. 8:1, 2 NIV). "For Christ did not enter a man-made sanctuary that was only a copy of the true one; he entered heaven itself, now to appear for us in God's presence" (Heb. 9:24, NIV).

Exactly what the image of a heavenly tabernacle means is not important to us at this point. One great fact is clear: Jesus Christ has entered the very presence of the holy God in our behalf, to present before Him the sacrifice that He Himself has made, and to plead that atonement for all who believe in Him. Not only has He done that—He does it now! "If anyone does sin, we have one who speaks to the Father in our defense—

Jesus Christ the righteous One. He is the atoning sacrifice for our sins" (1 John 2:1, 2, NIV).

Christ is alive! He is our Intercessor, our great High Priest this very hour. He prays for us right now; He pleads His sacrifice for us. This is why we can have a freed conscience day by day. The more we trust in Him, the more we know and walk with Him, the more we will rest in this.

In addition to Christ's resurrection, ascension, exaltation, and high priestly ministry, one more function of the living Christ must be considered. We sometimes give too little weight to the fact that Christ's requesting the Holy Spirit for us and then sending Him to us was also an integral part of His redemptive work and precisely in the heavenly sequence we have been considering.

In the seventh chapter of John's Gospel, against the beautiful backdrop of the ceremonies which climaxed the Feast of Tabernacles, Jesus made a powerful statement about Himself, and John adds an instructive explanation: "Jesus stood and said with a loud voice, 'If a man is thirsty, let him come to me and drink. Whoever believes in me, as the Scripture has said, streams of living water will flow from within him.' By this he meant the Spirit, whom those who believed in him were later to receive. Up to that time the Spirit had not been given, since Jesus had not yet been glorified" (John 7:37-39, NIV). Here "streams of living water" are quite simply the result of faith in Christ. But by the time John wrote this account, he was able to provide a clear explanation of what Jesus meant. He knew that Jesus had been speaking about the indwelling presence of the Holy Spirit in believers' lives. Even more remarkably, he knew that the initiating of this relationship with the Holy Spirit was connected with the exaltation of Christ.

Peter demonstrated this awareness on the Day of Pentecost. He brought his sermon that day to a climax with these words: "God has raised this Jesus to life, and we are all witnesses of the fact. Exalted to the right hand of God, he has received from the Father the promised Holy Spirit and has poured out what you now see and hear" (Acts 2:32, 33, NIV).

Jesus had predicted this also: "I will ask the Father, and He will give you another Counselor to be with you forever—the Spirit of truth" (John 14:16, NIV). It becomes clear that Jesus' asking occurred at the time of His exaltation and high priestly session in the presence of His Father.

One of the great summary statements of the effect of Christ's ministry was the prophecy of John the Baptist. He said that the coming One would "baptize . . . with the Holy Spirit and with fire" (Matt. 3:11, NIV). Here was the consummation of the Old Testament prophetic view of the Messiah. The great result of His work would be a far more intimate and complete relationship with the living Spirit of God than had been possible since sin destroyed the original fellowship in the Garden. Now Christ has completed His atoning work. He is alive in the presence of the Father. He has presented the sacrifice before the presence of God in behalf of His own. Now is the moment for Him to request and receive the gift of God's own presence for the lives of His people. No more tabernacles and temples with altars and sacrifices were necessary. God could now dwell in the very bodies of His people and make *them* His temple!

One significant conclusion to be drawn from this sequence of events has to do with the *tarrying* that Jesus commanded His disciples to do, between the time of His ascension and the Day of Pentecost. The disciples' tarrying cannot be made to teach a similar waiting period in Christians' experience after conversion—a kind of preparation of life for the coming of the Holy Spirit. Instead it had to do with the sequence of events taking place around Christ Himself. Without realizing it, perhaps, the disciples were waiting for Christ's exaltation to take place and His intercession before the Father to begin, a unique and never-to-be-repeated tarrying. The presence of the Holy Spirit with believers in the new and intimate way did not depend on their preparation, but on Christ's advocacy, as it does still.

Another important conclusion to be drawn from these insights is that the ministry of the Holy Spirit is not separate from the ministry of Christ in glory. He Himself made this clear to His disciples before He left them: "When he, the Spirit of truth comes, he will guide you into all truth. He will not speak on his own; he will speak only what he hears, and he will tell you what is yet to come. He will bring glory to me by taking from what is mine and making it known to you" (John 16:12-

14, NIV). "He will speak only what he *hears*"! This is a startling expression. It implies an intimate and continual interchange between the Spirit who indwells believers and the living, glorious Christ. It would be an error to suppose that Christ finished His activity and that the Holy Spirit then began His work. Christ is the living Head of His body, and He dwells within it by His Spirit. The Holy Spirit takes the graces and directions that come from the Head and administers them here on earth. This does not mean at all that the Holy Spirit is a lesser member of the Trinity, but rather that the whole Godhead is active in the application of redemption to our lives. The Holy Spirit brings heaven into our dismal scene and makes it the operating ground of the living Christ.

The sum of what we have been considering in the past two chapters is this: Salvation is in Jesus Christ. It is true that he represented us in the things that He did—identified Himself with us to become our sin-bearer and the conqueror of our ills. But the whole process and its results were uniquely worked out in His own Person and experience. He put away sin, death, and Satan from Himself and came out of the grave as the new man, totally on the other side of them all—beautiful, powerful, unique, and very much alive. He has been exalted at the right hand of the Father and possesses all the human attributes and freedom that we need and long for. He presents His claims to the Father in our behalf, and He has sent and continues to send the Holy

Spirit to us to animate His body here. He is the living and glorious head of His body.

The implication of this for us is that the extent to which our redemption will become a vital part of our experience will depend on our relationship to Him and the work of His Spirit within our lives. What has been secured and is complete in Him, and what is placed to our account immediately upon the exercise of faith in Christ, must be derived from Him in our experience.

But even while we long for more transference of His victory into our experience, we look with awe and love at the Christ who died for us according to the Scriptures, and who rose again the third day according to the Scriptures—the living Christ of glory. And we understand with new gratitude what exceedingly good news the dual message of the gospel is.

NINE

Union
with Christ

The preceding chapter left us with an exciting picture of Jesus Christ. He is alive from the dead. He is victorious over all human ills. He has all the virtue and power of that victory in His own Person. He has been exalted and glorified in the presence of the Father, where He is active in our behalf. He is on the other side of all our problems, possessing in Himself the solution to them. *But He has gone from our scene!*

Meanwhile we are still here in this evil world. Ungodliness surrounds us. We still have a nature which can rebel and declare its independence from God at the drop of a hat. This flesh is both within us and around us. There is death on every side, and even though we are partakers of life in Christ, we know too often the practical woe of spiritual deadness. We are still targets of the prowling lion, Satan, who organizes powerful resistance to our walk with God.

We are here; Jesus is there! We are full of needs; He

has all we need. It is obvious that our greatest need is to be in touch with the living Christ—to have a vital and effective contact by which His supply will touch our needs. This is precisely what the Bible says is true of us: we have been joined to Christ in a permanent, real, vital, and effective union. This has been true of us from the very moment of our faith in Him, and it provides us with the basis upon which many life-changing responses may be made.

Reconciliation to the Father is one of the main goals and results of the redemptive work of Christ. "God was reconciling the world to himself in Christ" (2 Cor. 5:19, NIV). Now much more specifically we are considering the unique relationship which is established between the believer and Christ Himself. The New Testament constantly witnesses to this fact. Believers are frequently spoken of as "in Christ"; they are said to have been "sealed in Christ," "baptized into Christ Jesus." "Christ in you the hope of glory" is called a gloriously rich mystery in Colossians 1:27 (NIV).

In addition to such language, the New Testament contains symbols and figures which represent this union. Marriage is used in this way, with Christ as the Groom and the Church as bride. The same relationship is suggested by the figure of a building of which Christ is the Cornerstone and His people the various parts, and also by the symbol of the Vine and its branches.

Is this relationship real, or are these scriptural expressions simply a graphic way of describing an ideal of the mind? We are, after all, living in the twentieth century, not the first. How can we possibly conceive of union with Jesus Christ as being real?

We have already taken a giant step toward this by recognizing that Christ Himself is alive and active—that somewhere in this universe Christ Himself exists in His resurrection body, the only example of a new humanity indeed, but genuine and contemporary. Both parties to the relationship, in other words, are real and current, and that opens up the possibility of a real union. If both parties are real, then the remaining question is whether or not there is a real "bridge" to connect the two.

Jesus Himself, knowing that His time for leaving the disciples was rapidly approaching, showed considerable interest in reassuring them at this point. Here are His words: "I will not leave you as orphans; I will come to you. Before long the world will not see me anymore, but you will see me. Because I live, you also will live. On that day you will realize that I am in my Father, and you are in me, and I am in you" (John 14:18-20, NIV). Note the clear promise that He would be in touch with them, and they with Him. They would actually share His life, and they would know the reality of this union.

Jesus is here teaching about the coming of the Holy Spirit. Just before the words, "I will not leave you as orphans," Jesus had promised to ask the Father to send them "another Counselor to be with you forever—the Spirit of truth" (verses 16, 17, NIV). He goes on to say, "The world cannot accept him, because it neither sees him nor knows him. But you know him, for he lives with you and will be in you." It is precisely at this point that Jesus says, "I will not leave you as orphans; I will come to you." And when He says, *"On that day* you will realize that . . . you are in me and I am in you," it is quite clear that He refers to the day when the Holy Spirit would be sent to them. The Holy Spirit *is* the "bridge." It is in His personal presence that we discern the living Christ and are bound to Him. Because the Holy Spirit is *real,* this is a real union.

In Romans 8:9-11, dealing with the indwelling presence of God in the believer, Paul gives five different names to this presence: "You, however, are controlled not by the sinful nature but by the Spirit, if the *Spirit of God* lives in you. And if anyone does not have the *Spirit of Christ,* he does not belong to Christ. But if *Christ* is in you, your body is dead because of sin, yet your spirit is alive because of righteousness. And if *the Spirit of him who raised Jesus from the dead* is living in you, he who raised Christ from the dead will also give life to your mortal bodies through *his Spirit,* who lives in you" (NIV, italics added). While the emphasis is on the Spirit in this passage, He is called the Spirit of God, the Spirit of Christ, the Spirit of Him who raised Jesus (i.e., the Father), or even just *Christ.*

Here is the mystery of the Trinity. Jesus said to Philip on one occasion, "Anyone who has seen me has seen the Father" (John 14:9, NIV). One member of the Trinity may be discerned in another. The Father may be discerned in the Son; both the Father and the Son may be discerned in the Spirit.

Consider also God's attribute of *omnipresence,* the fact that He is everywhere at once. The Holy Spirit is God and has this attribute also. It is perfectly correct to think of the Holy Spirit as present in the believer's life—indeed, the same Holy Spirit is simultaneously present in every believer's life—but He is also present with the living Christ in glory. In the preceding chapter we noted that remarkable statement about the Holy Spirit that "he will speak only *what he hears*" (John 16:13, NIV), as He takes the things of Christ and makes them real to us.

All of this underscores the fact that the very person of the Holy Spirit *is* the connection between us and Christ, and that this makes our union real, vital, and powerful. Union with Christ is not just an ideal, a thought, a manner of speaking. We are actually in touch with the Christ in whom all the answers to our problems have been fully secured. He is also in us by the presence of His Spirit. Indeed, He has not left us as orphans; we are not alone. Christ in us is the hope of glory.

One feature of this union with Christ that is deeply encouraging is its permanence. Christ said about the coming of the Holy Spirit that the Father "will give you another Counselor to be with you forever—the Spirit of truth." That He can be with us at all is dependent, not on our merit or state of personal righteousness, but on the atonement of Jesus Christ. It is the gift of Christ's righteousness that makes possible the presence of an absolutely holy God in sinful human beings. So also His continuance with us rests on the same ground and is therefore permanent. We may grieve Him, even quench His work. We may be in awesome bondage and spiritual decline. Yet He is still there, offering us His marvelous help and restoration. As Christians we never start from scratch in dealing with our difficulties. The Spirit of Christ is with us, and this means we are joined to Christ the Victor! Nothing can change this.

To call this union with Jesus Christ a *vital* union, is to emphasize the fact that it is full of life and vigor, full of vital interaction with the living Christ. By the Holy Spirit's presence, powerful life flows from the Head to the members of His body.

John begins his first epistle with a strong description of Jesus Christ as *life:* "What was from the beginning, what we have heard, what we have seen with our eyes, what we beheld and our hands handled, concerning the Word of life—and the life was manifested, and we have seen and bear witness and proclaim to you the eternal life, which was with the Father and was manifested to us" (1 John 1:1, 2, NASB). The Word, that is, Christ, is here called "the Word of life," indeed "eternal life" itself. John goes on to introduce the thought of sharing this life, using the beautiful New Testament word *koinonia* (fellowship). "What we have seen and heard we declare to you, so that you and we together may share in a common life, that life which we share with the Father and His Son Jesus Christ" (1 John 1:3, NEB).

It is no mere metaphor to say that we have the life of Christ in common! The presence of the Holy Spirit makes possible a vital flow from Christ to us that is real and powerful. Because of His presence in all the members of the body of Christ, this is a life which we have in common with each other as well, and this makes possible a powerful operation of the living Christ in the Christian community as well as in individual Christians.

Because the presence of the Holy Spirit is permanent in the lives of Christians, their union with each other is also permanent. One of the times when this can be most powerfully meaningful to us is the occasion of the "loss" of a Christian loved one. Actually, in the ultimate sense, Christians can never lose each other. Union with Christ continues unchanged through the experience of physical death. The Christian who has died is still joined to the same Christ, and so is the brother or sister who is left behind. "Neither death nor life . . . nor anything else in all creation, will be able to separate us from the love of God that is in Christ Jesus our Lord" (Rom. 8:38, 39, NIV).

Because of this vital union there can be the powerful implanting of the characteristics which abound in the new man, Jesus Christ. That these are called the "fruit of the Spirit" in no way obscures the fact that Christ is the source of them. Allowing the "fruit of the Spirit" to grow in our lives as Christians is precisely the same as obeying the command of Romans 13:14 to "put on the Lord Jesus Christ." The fruit of the Spirit passage in Galatians emphasizes the fact that love, joy, peace, and the other fruits of grace flow into our lives through the presence of the Holy Spirit, who takes the things of

Christ and makes them real to us. The Romans 13 passage calls attention to the Source, Jesus Christ, and to the fact that we have responsibility to lay claim to this process in our lives.

Through this same great "Bridge" the gifts of God come to us. Ephesians 4 describes the picture of the exalted Christ giving gifts to His body (verses 7-13), while 1 Corinthians 12 describes the way the Holy Spirit distributes gifts to Christians. This is no contradiction, nor are different processes in view. Whatever gifts are brought into the lives of Christians, these are secured in the Person of Jesus Christ for them and brought into their experience by the vital ministry of the Holy Spirit.

Union with Christ can have wonderful effects. We are not required to "pull ourselves up by our bootstraps"— to try in our own strength to imitate Christ. Though He is indeed our great Example, the means by which the pattern is reduplicated in us is participation in Christ rather than imitation alone. Union with Christ by the Holy Spirit's presence means that effective power can flow into us which is infinitely greater than our weakness. Union with Christ is the basis for all experience of godliness in our lives.

The Scriptures become quite specific in describing union with Christ. In this respect there is a distinct parallel with the twin centers of the gospel: the death and resurrection of Christ. There are a number of places where the Bible speaks of union with Christ, not simply in terms of a general union with His Person, but as a specific union with His death and with His resurrection.

Here we should remember a major emphasis of the preceding two chapters. The entire process of redemption was carried out within the scope of Jesus' Person. He was made sin for us; He entered the experience of death for every man; the human conflict with satanic powers became concentrated in his own Person at Calvary. And it was in His own Person that the results were achieved and reside in all their perfection and power. He is the one Man on the other side of the grave, the only Example of the new humanity, the only Man in glory. The virtue and power of each step of the redemptive process is fully present in Him: the mind to obey as man should obey, death to sin, life to God, freedom and power over all opposing powers, glory in restored fellowship with the Father. All these reside in perfection in the living Christ.

So Scripture speaks of union with Christ in His death: "Don't you know that all of us who were baptized into Christ Jesus were baptized into His death?" (Rom. 6:3, NIV). What this is saying in effect is that by our union with Christ we have been brought directly in touch with the power of His dying to sin!

Again the Word says, "You have been raised with Christ" (Col. 3:1, NIV). This is the other focus of the gospel. United to Christ we have been brought in touch with the virtue and power of His new life to God.

Romans 6:11 combines these thoughts in a single sentence: "In the same way, count yourselves dead to sin and alive to God in Christ Jesus" (NIV). In union with the living Christ we are brought into contact with both realities, His death and His resurrection life.

By far the most striking scriptural illustration of this truth is the one used at the beginning of Romans 7: "For the married woman is bound by law to her husband while he is living; but if her husband dies, she is released from the law . . . so that she is not an adulteress, though she is joined to another man. Therefore, my brethren, you also were made to die to the Law through the body of Christ, that you might be joined to another, to Him who was raised from the dead, that we might bear fruit for God" (verses 2-4, NASB). Here the phrase "through the body of Christ" makes it plain that Christ is symbolized by both the dead husband and the new, living husband in the illustration! The believer is spoken of as joined first to the Christ who died, so that then he might be joined to the Christ who rose from the dead. The virtue and power of both death and resurrection can flow into the Christian's life in union with Christ.

Why should Scripture make an emphasis like this? Would it not be sufficient to emphasize union with Christ in a general way, the Christ in whom all things are completed; in other words, union with the end product? Why, specifically, the emphasis on our union with Him in His dying to sin? The answer to this, of course, is that we are still in a condition where we need help in dying to sin, if we are to live to God. And this specific help abounds in Christ for us. It sounds strange indeed to say, but union with Christ puts us in touch with the *dynamic of death to sin*. Without this we could never walk in freedom with our God.

Another way to look at this holds in view the work the Holy Spirit sets out to do in us after entering our lives. He comes to us as God. He intends to express in us the sovereign right of God to rule. He intends to establish the lordship of Jesus Christ in our lives. But He encounters immediately our own "god-complex." "For the flesh sets its desire against the Spirit, and the Spirit against the flesh; for these are in opposition to one another" (Gal. 5:17, NASB). The Holy Spirit, therefore, intends to duplicate in us the redemptive sequence of death and resurrection, bringing to bear on us first the virtue and power of Christ's dying to sin and then the release of His resurrection life.

This process in our experience is specifically described in Philippians 3:10, 11: "That I may know Him [Christ], and the power of His resurrection and the fellowship of His sufferings, being conformed to His death, in order that I may attain to the resurrection from the dead" (NASB). "Being conformed to His death" translated literally is: *"becoming continually* conformed to His death"—a continuing action in the present. This makes it very plain that Paul is talking about an experiential way of "knowing Christ," a progressive experience of touching the power of Christ's dying to sin, so that an increasing experience of Christ's resurrection life may follow.

All of this is possible because of our union with

Christ. It provides a real connection, so that virtue and power can flow from Christ into our lives.

On the resurrection side of union with Christ, the Bible includes union with Him in the whole sequence following His emergence from the grave. Paul tells the Ephesians, "God raised us up with Christ and seated us with him in the heavenly realms in Christ Jesus" (Eph. 2:6, NIV); "Praise be to the God and Father of our Lord Jesus Christ, who has blessed us in the heavenly realms with every spiritual blessing in Christ" (Eph. 1:3, NIV). It will be the work of the Holy Spirit eventually to bring all of us who are His purchased possession into the full experience of these benefits, culminating in heaven itself. But even now, there are ever-increasing transfers of authority, power, glory, and fellowship with the Father which the Holy Spirit can bring into our lives in the midst of a dark world.

As we look at the New Testament Scriptures regarding union with Christ, it is quite plain that the understanding of this reality is intended to establish a basis upon which we can and must make certain responses and choices of faith. This is nothing more than a development of the overall call of the gospel, "Believe on the Lord Jesus Christ and you will be saved." We are not only called upon to *know* that we have been joined to Jesus in his death and resurrection, but we are instructed to *count* on this fact (Rom. 6:11). In fact, Romans 8:13 states the obligation even more actively: "If by the Spirit you put to death the misdeeds of the body, you will live" (NIV). This surely envisions the work of the

Holy Spirit in bringing the virtue and power of Christ's death and resurrection to us, but it also calls for an act of faith, an opting for the Holy Spirit's operation based on the reality of our union. And that is the point: because we are really bonded to Christ by the Holy Spirit, we have grounds for certain expectations of power in our lives and the basis for responses of faith that are increasingly accurate and effective. This is beginning to put in our hands tools of freedom which are more than adequate for coping with the severe problems we face. No enemy can withstand the Christian who by the Holy Spirit stands on his union with the living Christ!

TEN

The Holy Spirit and the Individual Believer

Jesus Christ was born of a woman, born a tiny human baby in humble circumstances. His humanity was evident then and throughout His earthly life. For His disciples, contact with Jesus brought about a steady growth in their understanding of his real identity. They became convinced that He was their Messiah, and Peter eventually gave voice to this conviction (Matt. 16:16). But the peak of their understanding was spoken not by Peter, but by Thomas after the resurrection. Finally convinced that Jesus was truly alive, he falls at His feet in worship and cries, "My Lord and my God" (John 20:28). These humble fishermen finally realized that the man with whom they had walked and talked throughout Galilee and Judea was the one true and living God, come in human flesh.

The same realization about the Holy Spirit had to grow in the Jerusalem church. Christ had promised a unique relationship with the Holy Spirit. They were to wait for this to be established. He had described the Spirit as "another Counselor," that is, another similar to Himself. They had gone through the experience of Pentecost and had known the touch of the Spirit's power through various evidences which must have been deeply moving to them. However, an incident soon occurred in the church that electrified and sobered every believer.

Under the direction of the Holy Spirit, a material emergency was being met by the sacrificial sale of property. Some Christians were selling their possessions and turning the entire proceeds over to the apostles for meeting the current need. Ananias and Sapphira, aware of this call, had also sold property and brought part of the proceeds to Peter. But they had agreed to pretend before the church that this represented total giving of their goods, when actually it did not. Peter was given insight to see their deception and rebuked them sharply. His words to Ananias were: "Ananias, how is it that Satan has so filled your heart that you have lied to the Holy Spirit? . . . You have not lied to men but to God!" (Acts 5:3, 4, NIV). Ananias, at this rebuke, fell dead before Peter, and later Sapphira met the same end. Scripture reports that "great fear seized all who heard what had happened"; and again, "Great fear seized the whole church" (Acts 5:5, 11, NIV).

They were made shockingly aware that in the presence of the Holy Spirit, their one true and living God had come to them in an immediacy never before known. They began to walk softly before God. This mood prevailed for a long time. In Acts 9, the tenor of their life is described in these words: "So the church throughout all Judea and Galilee and Samaria enjoyed peace, being built up; and going on in the fear of the Lord and in the comfort of the Holy Spirit, it continued to increase" (Acts 9:31, NASB).

As the Old Testament prophets had looked forward to the times of the Messiah, many times they said that God was going to enter into a close, unique relationship with His people in messianic times. Sometimes there is merely the statement, "You will be my people, and I will be your God" (Jer. 30:22; 32:38, NIV). Sometimes there is reference to a new covenant that God would make with His people at that time: "The time is coming, declares the Lord, when I will make a new covenant with the house of Israel. . . . This is the covenant I will make . . . after that time, declares the Lord. I will put my law in their minds and write it on their hearts. I will be their God, and they will be my people. No longer will a man teach his neighbor, or a man his brother, saying, Know the Lord, because they will all know me, from the least of them to the greatest, declares the Lord" (Jer. 31:31-34, NIV). The implication here is that the knowledge of the Lord would not only be more widespread among His people, but perhaps more intimate as well.

This idea is made more explicit in Ezekiel's prophecy: "I will sprinkle clean water on you and you will be clean. . . . I will give you a new heart and put a new spirit in you. . . . I will put my Spirit in you. . . . You will be my people, and I will be your God" (Ezek. 36:25-28, NIV; see also Ezek. 11:19, 20). This is the high point of Old Testament prophecy of this nature.

What is already clear in the Old Testament is that God's promised relationship under the New Covenant would be fulfilled by the presence of the Holy Spirit in believers' hearts. When John the Baptist summed up the whole ministry that the Christ would have, he simply said, "He will baptize you with the Holy Spirit." This would be God present with His people in the New Covenant way. It would be the great result of Messiah's work.

All that we have been saying in this book regarding God's design to have fellowship with His people, the human independency which resists and mars this design, and the purpose of redemption to rebuild that fellowship comes to a focus now in our relationship with the Holy Spirit.

All Christians need to grow in the experience of their fellowship with the Holy Spirit—God in them. This is indicated by the four direct commands given to Christians regarding the Holy Spirit: "Do not quench the Spirit" (1 Thess. 5:19, NASB); "Do not grieve the Holy Spirit of God" (Eph. 4:30, NIV); "Be filled with the Spirit" (Eph. 5:18, NIV); and "Walk by the Spirit" (Gal. 5:16, 25, NASB). These commands to Christians would have no meaning at all if it were not possible for Christians to walk contrary to them. In other words, it has to be possible for Christians to grieve and quench the Spirit, to be something less than filled with the Holy

Spirit, and to fail to walk by the Spirit. This, of course, fits the picture previously drawn of our flesh and its opposition to anything or anyone that threatens its autonomy. The command of Scripture to grow in grace and in the knowledge of Christ should be understood to call centrally for growth in fellowship with the Spirit of God, since He is the One by whom grace and the knowledge of Christ come to us.

Communion (sharing of life) with the Holy Spirit is genuine fellowship. It is the interaction of God and man, just as truly as is the fellowship we have with the Father and with Jesus Christ. As we said earlier, fellowship is two-sided. It involves the function of whole beings interacting with each other. To think of fellowship with the Holy Spirit as something always operating beneath the level of our consciousness, something automatic, or involving no awareness of Him, is an insult to *His* personhood. To think of it as an experience in which He becomes so overwhelming as to wipe out our self-awareness or integrity of function is an insult to *our* personhood. Jesus apparently had something of this sort in mind when He assured His disciples concerning the Holy Spirit that they *knew* Him, "for he lives with you and will be in you" (John 14:17, NIV). Redemption was designed to provide the reality of God-living-with-man and man-living-with-God, a relationship of love and personal integrity on both sides.

If the experience of such fellowship is to grow, how are we to seek this growth? This is an important question. Even as Christians we are vulnerable to extremes.

The prospect of "knowing the Holy Spirit" may fill some with such enthusiasm that they become very subjective and unstable in their approach. They may easily fall prey to impulses that they are sure come from the Holy Spirit, but which are actually of their own contriving; or worse, the contrivings of an alien spirit. Others, of a more rationalistic bent, fearful of anything that might in any way partake of such enthusiasm, will rigidly rule out any direct awareness of the Spirit of God at all. In either case the result is the same: loss of fellowship with God. Our adversary probably cares little which of these ways we go, so long as that is the result.

A marvelously simple and direct instruction concerning growth in the knowledge of the Holy Spirit was given by John Calvin. In his *Instruction in Faith* of 1537, he gave an exposition of the Apostles' Creed. When he came to the statement in the creed, "I believe in the Holy Ghost," Calvin said, "When we are taught to believe in the Holy Spirit, we are also commanded to expect from Him what is said about Him in the Scripture" (Calvin, *Instruction In Faith*, 1537, Fuhrmann translation, Westminster Press, 1949, p. 51). Here is a balanced and safe principle to follow. When the Bible clearly teaches that the Holy Spirit is present with us to perform certain functions, we should seek with faith the enlarging of those experiences in our lives. We should invoke His aid along the lines in which that aid has been promised.

A crucial area in which the Holy Spirit's aid is promised and much needed is the handling of the independency of our flesh. "If *by the Spirit* you put to death the misdeeds of the body, you will live" (Rom. 8:13, NIV). This is certainly a promise of the Holy Spirit's aid! The only alternate understanding of this promise is unthinkable: as though somehow we can, at our pleasure rather than His, *use* the Holy Spirit in overcoming the evil of our nature. No one *uses* God! Rather, this is an aid which the Holy Spirit gives and which we should seek.

In fact, it is most encouraging to realize that the Holy Spirit who has come to live in us is already "in motion" with the aid that we need. Concerning our flesh, Paul said, "The flesh sets its desire against the Spirit, *and the Spirit against the flesh.*" There may be internal war going on here, but it is not a one-sided war. The Holy Spirit is already in action against our flesh. We do not have to "twist His arm" to get Him going for our help in this area! Nor in the matter of our need for help in prayer do we need to plead with Him to get off dead center and help us pray. He is already interceding within us "with groanings too deep for words" (Rom. 8:26, NASB).

Here is a marvel! The Spirit taking up residence in new believers finds in them a deeply entrenched "god-complex" which resists the Spirit's right to rule. But the Holy Spirit Himself is ready and able, in fact, already moving powerfully, to bring into the situation the virtue and power of Christ's dying to sin. The Holy Spirit aids in clearing away the opposition to Himself. But there is a fellowship to be had with Him even in this process. Our assent and claim of faith is required: a deliberate choice to go in this direction. Even in this choice, we may seek His help, recognizing our dependence on His power.

The process by which our independency is replaced by fellowship with the Holy Spirit is an extensive one. The depth to which the flesh permeates all areas and functions of our life requires an equally broad and deep application of "dying" with Christ, if we are to experience our freedom. During all of our present existence we will be learning the subtleties of the operation of our flesh—in mental habits, emotional binds, characteristic independency in the expression of our sexuality, rebellions of the will, and so on. This is not to be a nit-picking, self-organized ferreting out of sin, but one of our most important areas of fellowship with the Holy Spirit. That fellowship will grow strongly. More and more place will be made for Him as the opposition to Him is brought under control. Also we will know Him better in the very process of counting on and receiving His help.

A much neglected passage in James is crucially relevant to our sanctification. In many translations of James 4:1-7, one looks in vain for any reference to the Holy Spirit. But He is there, and in a most striking way. Translators have had much difficulty with verse 5. NIV gives this reading: "Do you think Scripture says without reason that the spirit he caused to live in us tends toward envy?" "Tends toward envy" is too weak for the force of the word in the original language. The word is actually a strong verb for "longing" or "yearning." "Unto envy" or "unto jealousy" shows the measure or direction of the longing. The clause, "whom he caused to live in us" is clearly an identification of the Holy Spirit, whom God caused to dwell in us. These features make the margin reading in NIV preferable: "the Spirit he caused to live in us longs jealously." This verb of longing is used elsewhere in the New Testament eight times, always in a good sense, always in a distinctively Christian setting, and always in connection with a separation that ideally should be overcome. So Paul "longs" to see the Christians at Rome (Rom. 1:11); he "longs" for his heavenly dwelling (2 Cor. 5:2); Christians should "crave" their spiritual food (1 Peter 2:2). Such a longing would not be inappropriately applied to the Holy Spirit. But what does this mean: "The Spirit whom he caused to live in us longs jealously"?

The preceding context makes this sharply clear. Verses 1-3 vigorously describe the "flesh" at work in these Christians to whom James writes. It causes fights and quarrels that come "from your desires that battle within you" (NIV). It ruins prayer by supplying wrong motives for asking. Then in verse 4 comes a scathing denunciation. James literally calls them "adulteresses" and goes on to describe how friendship with the world is hatred toward God. What he then says is that such a walk in the flesh, with love toward the world, is violating the relationship which has been established between believers and the Holy Spirit, whom God has caused to live in them. To say that this makes Him "yearn" jealously is simply another way of describing the "grieving" of the Holy Spirit. He longs for His rightful place in the Christian. He longs for the fellowship and exclusive interactions of God with man. To think of the sovereign God yearning for a place that belongs to Him is strange indeed, but it is not inconsistent with the whole tenor of Scripture. It is a New Testament equivalent of His earlier cry: "All day long I have held out my hands to an obstinate people" (Isa. 65:2, NIV). James 4:7 tells Christians what to do about this situation in their lives: "Submit yourselves, then, to God. Resist the devil and he will flee from you" (NIV). In context we would understand "God" to refer to the indwelling Spirit of God, and we are here told to get on with the process by which He is enthroned in our lives. Only as that is done can we with a sure hand turn and face the evil one, who gained ground in us through our fleshly activity and worldliness. In this passage are all the elements that oppose godliness, plus a yearning Spirit who deserves free access to all our being.

The curbing of our independency and rebellion is a process by which we enter into practical fellowship with the Spirit of God in our thinking, in our feelings, in our wills, and in all the functions of our personalities. We must be mindful that such fellowship is constantly built by the impact of Scripture on our lives, and that prayer will be an active dimension of it. The Word will be used by the Holy Spirit as a mirror and convicting agent to reveal to us the reality of our needs, the areas in which our flesh operates still, and the responses of faith that we are to make, all the while quickening our awareness of God Himself. Prayer will be the normal way in which we make these responses.

Right here the question should be raised concerning the appropriateness of addressing prayer directly to the Holy Spirit. Sometimes the argument will be advanced that Scripture nowhere teaches that the Holy Spirit should be addressed directly, and that therefore this kind of prayer is wrong. To think this way is to fail to grasp the significance of the Trinity. The Holy Spirit is not one third of God; nor are there three Gods. The Holy Spirit is our one true and living God; He is all of God. Everything that is true of God is true of Him; everything that is due God in terms of worship, submission, dependence, and prayer is due the Holy Spirit. All that constitutes fellowship with God is to be true of fellowship with the Holy Spirit. It is inconceivable and unscriptural to tell believers that they may not pray to their God. If the Bible teaches prayer at all, it teaches prayer to the Holy Spirit.

This does not mean that a believer can rightly ignore the special significances attached to the unique operations of each member of the Godhead. Prayers may often be directed in harmony with some scripturally described function of one of the persons of the Trinity. It is inconceivable that a Christian would never directly thank Jesus Christ for His atonement at Calvary, nor seek His operation as Head of the Church through prayers addressed to Him. He is our God; He is alive; we are united to Him.

In the same way it is inconceivable that we be

forbidden to invoke the Holy Spirit concerning specific functions that Scripture ascribes to Him. Since the Word tells us *by the Spirit* to put to death the misdeeds of the body, it will be most appropriate for us to call on Him for this work in our lives. The process of honoring and enthroning Him as we die more and more to sin will be strengthened greatly by addressing our invitation to Him directly and personally. He is our one true and living God, come to live in us and do these very things.

Growth in fellowship with the Holy Spirit—in truly knowing Him—will come about through our expectation of all the ministries the Scripture ascribes to Him. Since the Bible says that He is the "anointing that teaches" (1 John 2:27), we should expect that kind of help, expect that He is already in motion in that direction and desires our responsive prayer toward that end. He is described as "taking hold with our weakness," particularly in the matter of prayer (Rom. 8:26, 27). How very appropriate it will be, then, as we approach prayer, to declare to Him our dependence on Him for this aid, and to expect it from Him. Scripture indicates that the Holy Spirit in us is greater than "he that is in the world" (1 John 4:4). As we enter into battle with the satanic kingdom, which according to Scripture we surely will (Eph. 6:10ff, for example), how marvelously encouraging it will be to us to declare our dependence on God the Holy Spirit to make the victory of Christ real in the given situation. This is grace at work. This is our response to grace; our stated dependence on grace. It is fellowship with the Spirit of God. The Bible teaches us to expect from the Holy Spirit the distribution of the gifts sent from Christ to His body (Eph. 4:7-13; 1 Cor. 12). It will be important to acknowledge our dependence on Him for this ministry as well, to call for and expect enlarged fellowship with Him in the matter of our gifts.

An area of much consequence to us, as we grow in fellowship with the Spirit of God, will become the subject of the next chapter. This involves growth of our fellowship and awareness of the Spirit of God in other members of the Christian community, surely an area worth much attention from Christians today.

A question often arises in discussing the growth of our relationship with the Holy Spirit: is this primarily brought about through a crisis experience, or is it a process which continues to take place in a believer's life? This manner of asking the question may in itself be misleading, since it implies an "either-or" situation. That there may be crises in our growth is evident. Particularly in the experience of fellowship with the Spirit of God, this is understandable. Even though our inheritance in Christ is all put to our account at conversion, and the presence of the Holy Spirit is a reality from that point, we may well be sadly unaware of the kind of opposition our flesh sets up to this fellowship. When we realize this and begin to make scripturally instructed responses, there may well be a great leap in our experience of the Holy Spirit. To some the idea of "knowing" the Holy Spirit, the idea that He is God and a real Person, the idea that there is such a thing as "the communion of the Holy Spirit" may burst on their awareness with radical consequences for their lives and their sense of fellowship with Him. Coming to expect the things that Scripture says about Him should indeed bring marked improvement in our experience of these things, since faith is the atmosphere in which God-awareness is nurtured. All of these developments may cause large or small crises along the way.

On the other hand, Scripture is abundantly plain that no crisis experience is anything more than a marked step in a process which is to develop all our lives. An instructive study may be made of the passages in Acts where the "filling" or "fullness" of the Spirit are mentioned. One group of these references clearly notes special crisis occasions when some ministry of the Spirit was much needed and was given. Peter and John stood before the council in Acts 4 to answer for their miraculous healing of the lame man. Then Peter, "filled with the Holy Spirit" is enabled to give a marvelously bold answer to them. The tense of the verb clearly indicates an "on-the-spot" filling by the Holy Spirit to meet this demand. The same kind of thing happened to Paul when the new missionary party was confronted by Elymas the sorcerer in Acts 13:9. Here Paul is "filled with the Holy Spirit" in an identical "on-the-spot" way and deals powerfully with his opponent.

However, when the apostles call on the church in Acts 6 to select helpers for the tasks of the church, they describe them as "men from among you who are known to be full of the Spirit and wisdom" (Acts 6:3,

NIV). Here the fullness of the Holy Spirit is not a sudden event, but a condition existing over a period of time, the effects of which could be observed in the wisdom of these men. So Barnabas similarly is called a "good man, full of the Holy Spirit and faith" (Acts 11:24, NIV). The first missionaries, after suffering persecution and expulsion from several places, are described in Acts 13:51 as "filled with joy and with the Holy Spirit" (NIV). This is not an "on-the-spot" tense of the verb, but one which indicates a continuing process. As they went through the experiences of hard labors and persecutions, they were growing in their fellowship with the Holy Spirit, and the fruit of it was joy.

The command of Ephesians 5:18 to be "filled with the Spirit" is also in a continuing form: literally, "Be being filled with the Spirit." There is to be a lifelong growth of our fellowship with God within.

How very easy it is to mar the experience of fellowship with the Spirit of God! Obviously, walking in the flesh will do that, causing grief and yearning on His part. We can mar the reality of fellowship by thinking of the Holy Spirit as an impersonal force—an "it," rather than the living God who is just as personal as we are. We can mar our fellowship by thinking of the Holy Spirit as a sort of inferior member of the Trinity who never calls attention to Himself, but only to Christ, and operates behind the scenes rather than as the living God dwelling in us. We can so magnify the crisis kind of experiences with Him that we ignore the daily process of getting to know Him better in the functions of life.

We will seriously mar our experience of fellowship with the Holy Spirit if we neglect Scripture and its role in building experience. Or we may mar our experience of fellowship with the Spirit of God by simple unbelief—not believing that He will actually do those things that Scripture says to expect from Him.

"Now may the God of hope fill you with all joy and peace in believing, that you may abound in hope by the power of the Holy Spirit" (Rom. 15:13, NASB).

ELEVEN

The Holy Spirit and the Christian Community

In the quaint and marvelous language of the King James Bible, David's vision of what the temple should be is recorded: "The house that is to be builded for the Lord must be exceeding magnifical, of fame and glory throughout all countries" (1 Chron. 22:5). And such surely was the magnificence and fame of Solomon's temple.

Now in God's providence and plan there are no temples made with hands in which God lives with his people. Under the New Covenant His presence with His people has become far more intimate than such structures would allow. Every individual believer is now a temple of God (1 Cor. 6:19), with the potential of displaying in a dark world something of the glory and beauty of the triumphant Christ. We ought to love that thought. And it is the presence of God Himself, the Holy Spirit, that can begin to clothe this temple with the magnificence of Christ. God's dwelling place surely should be touched with glory!

The Holy Spirit's shared presence in all believers also creates a larger temple. The same Holy Spirit indwells each believer at the same time. He lives in you; He lives in me; He lives in that unknown believer on the other side of the world. His presence creates a spiritual bond of union among all true Christians. In Christ "the whole building is joined together and rises to become a holy temple in the Lord. And in him you too are being built together to become a dwelling in which God lives by his Spirit" (Eph. 2:21, 22, NIV). We ought also to be deeply moved by the importance of this corporate temple, the Christian community—earnestly concerned that it, too, show the magnificence and beauty of its Head. To see its growth should be one of our greatest longings. The blemishes that mar its beauty and unity should be a strong grief to us.

It is not God's intention that the magnificence of the Church should be seen only at the end of history, when she is presented as a perfected bride to the Lord. Jesus said to the Father about His own, "I have given them the glory that you gave me, that they may be one as we are one: I in them and you in me. May they be brought to complete unity to let the world know that you sent me and have loved them even as you have loved me" (John 17:22, 23, NIV). The touch of Jesus' glory on the Church is designed to unite His people now and present a witness to the world of what Christ has done. This was something immensely dear to Jesus' own heart, and should be to ours.

The importance of the Christian community, indwelt by the Spirit of Christ, is emphasized to us by several scriptural themes. The Church finds her place in the kingdom emphasis of the Bible. Already David's greater Son is taking His kingdom to Himself and rules among His people. How important for the Christian community to display His great Lordship! The societal purposes of God, shown by God in the original creation and so dreadfully marred by sin and mocked by the existence of an intricate but godless world structure, are now reconstituted in the new humanity that believers share. Here is where long-lost purposes are to be revived and displayed.

The importance of the corporate life of the Christian community is also underscored by the fact that here in a unique manner we can know our God. For example, Matthew 18 speaks about corporate prayer in these terms: "If two of you agree on earth about anything that they may ask, it shall be done for them by My Father who is in heaven. For where two or three have gathered together in My name, there I am in their midst" (Matt. 18:19, 20, NASB). Each of these believers, before coming together, is individually united to Christ and is a temple of His Spirit. But when they come together in Christ's name, according to Christ's statement here, they have a unique awareness of His presence, a community way of discerning and knowing

Him. It is more than simply a matter of each individual in the group knowing the Lord and His help while together; there will be a group consciousness of Christ, a strengthening and harmonizing of prayer, an experience of God which can only be had in community.

It is by the Holy Spirit's presence that this potential exists. He is the One whose presence in each believer not only creates union with the living Christ, but the union of all believers. The same qualities that describe our individual union with Jesus Christ by the Spirit's presence also describe our union with each other. It is a real union, an effective union, a permanent union. It is a real union, because the Holy Spirit is real. The "body of Christ" is not some figurative or ideal concept. It exists in reality because the Holy Spirit has come to all believers. We do not have to attempt to *create* unity among Christians; it exists by the very nature of spiritual union. What we need rather is to learn to overcome the divisive characteristics which our own nature brings into the picture, and to learn to express and experience the unity which God has created. The relationship exists, however marred.

Such a perspective is clear in Paul's words to the Ephesians: "Be completely humble and gentle; be patient, bearing with one another in love. Make every effort to keep the unity of the Spirit in the bond of peace. There is one body and one Spirit—just as you were called to one hope when you were called—one Lord, one faith, one baptism, one God and Father of all, who is over all, and through all, and in all" (Eph. 4:2-6, NIV).

The bond between believers is a vital and effective bond because of the Holy Spirit. It is His shared presence that results in shared *life* (koinonia), and it is His sovereign and limitless power which can make our union effective. Our hope for the magnificence of the Church rests on the Holy Spirit's gracious work.

The union of Christians is a permanent union, because the presence of the Holy Spirit is permanent. This ought to produce a deep desire not to be at odds with any other person or group in whom the same Spirit of Christ lives. How much it must grieve the Savior, who prayed that the touch of His glory would draw His people together, to see the violent antagonisms and divisions that afflict His body. We should share this grief. While there are doubtless many situations in which the expression of unity may be presently impossible, we must in sheer faith recognize that unity exists, and prayerfully press for the removing of these impasses. We should labor at those points where He gives us hope that progress may be made. The Scriptures also reveal principles for promoting unity, approaches that can be made in the Spirit, ways of operating that neither violate conscience nor obliterate love and care.

It is the Holy Spirit's role to produce fruit in the lives of Christians, fruit that will promote healing and build the experience of unity. We have only to think of the items that are named as "fruit of the Spirit" to realize how true this is: "love, joy, peace, patience, kindness, goodness, faithfulness, gentleness, and self-control" (Gal. 5:22, 23). No situation is hopeless when this kind of fruit is appearing. Miraculous? Indeed! Impossible? Not at all! "Impossible" is not a word to be spoken in the presence of the almighty Spirit of God, especially when the Bible tells us to expect this fruit from Him.

Let us keep in mind that the completed work of Jesus Christ included His conquering the divisive sins and situations of mankind, His "slaying the enmity between Jew and Gentile" (Eph. 2:16). It is the virtue and power of this accomplishment that the Holy Spirit can bring into our human scene to cause the Christian community to stand together as "one new man."

It is the Holy Spirit's role to create a beautiful functioning of the Christian community by administering differing but complementary gifts, both to individual believers and, I'm convinced, to groups of Christians as well. When this ministry of the Holy Spirit is allowed free rein, the building really begins to take on magnificence. No task then lacks skillful and powerful workers to add creative and beautiful touches to the temple of God.

Seeing that the Holy Spirit's role is vital to the existence and function of the Christian community, how then shall we undertake to "keep the unity of the Spirit in the bond of peace"? There are two dimensions of the answer to this question: a personal and a corporate dimension.

On the personal level, it is obvious that the spiritual state of the individual strongly influences the functioning of groups. When one person acts "in the flesh," there is a tendency for responses to be made in the flesh by others. We must hope and pray for growth in the person who characteristically originates such discord. But it is also possible for the offended Christians to learn the discipline of the Holy Spirit so that they do not respond to such outbursts in kind. A soft answer still turns away wrath, and love still covers a multitude of sins (Prov. 15:1; 1 Pet. 4:8).

God's people must grow in their fellowship with Christ and so begin to share His outlook on other Christians. We must have fellowship with Him in His forgiving character. This forgiveness then can be prompt and unmerited. His character of love for His own must be implanted in us by the Holy Spirit, with all that this will mean in terms of unconditional acceptance, noticing, caring, burden-bearing, and encouragement. His joy over His own can become ours too and create an atmosphere of mutual delight in each other. Patience, kindness, gentleness, long-suffering, a willingness to risk the consequences of kindly rebukes given for the well-being of a fellow-Christian: these will all be a part of the scene where Christ reigns in individuals. The impact on community life will be great.

There is a corporate level of sanctification as well. There are community levels of flesh and sin. Groups of Christians go on ego trips too. Party spirit, pride of organization, exclusiveness, and evil actions can be displayed by groups as well as by individuals. Somehow we tend to feel that if we love each other within our group, this will be enough. We will not need to express as a group a loving, caring, sharing, and interacting spirit toward other Christian groups. This attitude is especially easy to fall into when our basis of understanding our group unity has been made to depend on our crossing our t's and dotting our i's in exactly the same way rather than on the shared life of the Holy Spirit. The Christian Church today is plagued by a great deal of this kind of separatism. In chapter two of this book we spoke of the crucial role that scriptural truth has in producing fellowship with God. For this reason various strong displays of that truth may serve the Church well. Fortunately, however, it is not only churches which subscribe to the Thirty-nine Articles, or the Heidelberg Catechism, or the Westminster Confession of Faith, in which the Holy Spirit lives. Basic fellowship among Christians, while needing truth to exist, is not created by adherence to these particular standards or any others, but by the shared presence of the Holy Spirit.

Corporate sins will mar our corporate fellowship with God and will require group repentance and re-honoring of the Holy Spirit in our midst. We will need to experience many forms of fellowship with God that involve each other: worshiping together, praise and singing, group prayer, joint fellowship in decision-making, and ministering together with a full display of the Spirit's varied gifts. This and more will occur in our shared relationship with the Holy Spirit, and these He Himself will enable.

For the initiating and sustaining of all the corporate life of the Church it is important that there be continued community use of the means of grace, especially joint study of the Word and group prayer at all levels of interaction. This is more than merely a convenient way for individuals to study the Bible or pray; it is part of the manner in which the group comes to experience intimacy with God.

God has established certain structures by which corporate segments of His body are to function. The local church, for example, has a biblical pattern for organizing its life. It is not easy to learn to function structurally in the Spirit. The exercise of watchcare by elders or other leaders to whom that function has been given by the Holy Spirit is a case in point (cf. Acts 20:28). Our human tendency is to abandon the powerful instruments of the Holy Spirit—the Word, prayer, love, example, warfare against Satan, united following of the Holy Spirit in decision-making—and stoop to simple legalism. When the Holy Spirit is honored and knowledgably followed by elders, this will be unnecessary in the vast majority of situations. Responsibility will always have to be taken, care given, admonitions offered and received, respect and support given, but simply resorting to the weight of authority is far below the privileges of a Christian operation.

The same is true of the family structure. Here the husband/father is the elder in this smallest unit of the

Church. He bears responsibility before God for the welfare of his family. However, if it is a Christian marriage, the two have opportunity for joint submission to the Lord Christ and of knowing His Spirit together. They, like the rest of the Church, may jointly be led by Him, may enter into joint prayer and decision-making. They can enjoy shared functions, mutual respect, and the power of love in such a way that a legalistic display of headship will be unnecessary and far beneath Christian privileges. This is no dishonoring of God-ordained structures, but simply an acknowledgment of the power of the spiritual dynamics within the Christian community.

Peter's instruction is applicable to both spheres mentioned above: "To the elders among you, I appeal as a fellow-elder. . . . Be shepherds of God's flock that is under your care, serving as overseers—not because you must, but because you are willing, as God wants you to be; not greedy for money, but eager to serve; not lording it over those entrusted to you, but being examples to the flock" (1 Peter 5:1-3, NIV). Only the Holy Spirit can work the miracles that will make these balances possible.

When we think of the community of God's people, it is worth asking: just how much magnificence, how much beauty does God intend His Church to display? We must realize that in setting up this oasis in an evil world, He is causing to intrude on the old scene the character of Christ in glory, the new creation, the new humanity. In 1 Corinthians 15, the resurrection chapter, it is implied that the new creation is to the old as the full flower is to the bare seed (cf. 1 Cor. 15:35-49). When one looks at the beauties that may be seen in this old-order world, such a concept is breathtaking. But when we look at the risen, exalted, and gloriously beautiful Savior, and think that we have been united to Him even while we are on this side of the grave, we know that the glory which He wants us to display must indeed be of the highest order: "For what was glorious has no glory now in comparison with the surpassing glory. And if what was fading away came with glory, how much greater is the glory of that which lasts!" (2 Cor. 3:10, 11, NIV).

The Holy Spirit, God present among us, has come to prepare a bride for Christ. "Christ loved the church and gave himself up for her to make her holy, cleansing her by the washing of water through the word, and to present her to himself as a radiant church, without stain or wrinkle or any other blemish, but holy and blameless" (Eph. 5:25-27, NIV). We have much to learn as we fellowship with the Holy Spirit in this task.

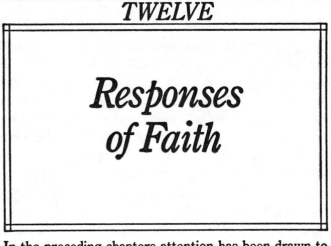

TWELVE

Responses of Faith

In the preceding chapters attention has been drawn to the essential teachings of the Bible about life with God. These principles provide a solid basis for growth in the experience of Christianity. In this final chapter we want to focus on the *how* of appropriation. How should a believer in Christ respond to all this?

First, let us remind ourselves of what we have seen so far. God designed us for fellowship with Himself. In so doing, He also designed and made possible fellowship with each other on the human level. Sin wrought terrible havoc in both areas of fellowship. Redemption is to be understood as providing for the healing of both relationships. Christians, however, though justified in God's sight, accepted in Christ, and made the dwellingplace of the Holy Spirit, still encounter much difficulty both in walking with God and with each other. This difficulty arises in part from the fact that we are material-spiritual beings seeking to walk with the Infinite Spirit, and therefore we must set apart special times for nourishing this spiritual relationship. More specifically, our difficulty arises from the fact that human nature is still characterized by rebellion and independency, which permeate all functions of our personalities. Behind this, and utilizing it as often as he can within God's sovereign control is Satan, the original rebel and historical source of independency. All of these factors combine to produce a godless world system, a false kingdom, where flesh runs rampant and Satan is the coordinator—a setting in which Christians are to shine brightly as proof of Christ's triumph.

The good news of Christ has a double focus: the death and resurrection of Jesus. Of great importance to us is the fact that the entire human problem was solved within the sphere of Christ's own person, as the second and last Adam. He obeyed actively for us; in His death He encompassed all our rebellion and sin, all our death and separation, all the satanic tyranny to which the human race had fallen prey. In His own Person He brought these factors down into death and thus ended them, so far as His own representative involvement with them was concerned. Even the world system is spoken of as judged and crucified with Christ. The consequence of this is that Christ came out of the grave as the beginning of a new order. A new creation now exists in Him; a new humanity in which all that afflicted the old has passed away. Salvation is fully present in the living Person of Christ. He ascended to the Father to present his sacrifice in our behalf, to receive His glory both as God and man. He is there now in His resurrection body and life, our Advocate, the Head of His body. He asked for and received the gift of the Holy Spirit for us. He is King over all. All that we need is in Christ, fully accomplished and perfected.

The Holy Spirit's very presence in believers joins them to Christ in a real, vital, effective, and permanent union. We are also joined similarly to all other believers by His shared presence. The virtue and power of all that Christ possesses in His own Person can now touch our experience, individually and collectively. This union places us in touch with Christ's dying to sin and His living to God, and becomes the ground for our expectation of help and for the kind of faith responses that we are to make. The Holy Spirit deals with our independency problem by conforming us to Christ's dying. We, however, have responsibility to choose this process and cooperate with it. As Satan's door of access to our experience is closed off, he may be resisted in the authority of Christ and made to flee from us. We have responsibility to act in faith in this dimension also. The Holy Spirit is to be enthroned in all parts and functions of our lives. He is also able to bring to bear on the Christian community Christ's healing of divisions, as Christians honor and enthrone Him corporately. The Holy Spirit is God with us and in us, and here is where fellowship takes place in our experience.

These principles have been set forth with much attention to Scripture. The desire has not been to "proof-text" our ideas, but rather to place before the reader the very instrument that the Holy Spirit uses to produce faith. If these teachings of the Word have been considered prayerfully, a picture of God the Father, of Christ the Savior, and of the Holy Spirit should be emerging which fills the heart with hope. There are realities here on which our faith can stand! If all has been accomplished in Christ, if we are in touch with Christ, if the Spirit of God is in us to make all this real—if indeed God is *for* us in this way—then we can respond in faith, as directed by the Scriptures, and expect results to come!

These last statements are important indeed! It is often thought that just as soon as an attempt is made to describe the "faith handles" which are to accompany the experience of redemption, we divert attention from the sovereign provision of grace by God. Is this not a typical American "how to" trip, the easy mentality of providing a humanistic formula which will make everything automatically work?

It is not the intention of this chapter to do that. Rather, we are grounding what we say on the fact that Scripture plainly calls for faith responses to the gospel. The message of the Church has always been, "Believe on the Lord Jesus Christ, and you will be saved." Scripture is our rule for faith *and life,* and we can approach it with the confidence that part of its truth will be its revelation of the character of our faith responses. Central to the preceding chapters of this book has been the attempt to understand in a more particular way the essence of the gospel of Christ. If this has been done with accuracy, then it has prepared the way for more particular and accurate responses of faith, which are nothing more than believing the gospel.

In the following paragraphs, we will suggest actual wordings for prayers. These are not to be considered as mechanical formulas. They rather reflect the fact that prayers need to achieve an objective form, and they are examples of what such prayers might sound like. Use whatever words the Spirit of God gives you, but *do* respond with accuracy as the Scripture directs.

All right, what are the handles? What are the "take-hold" points? How do we go about this?

First, let us remember that the Holy Spirit is here to help us at every step. He is already in motion in the directions we need to go. At every point we can remind ourselves of His role by simply asking Him for His help. Since our responses are ordinarily first made by prayer, the petitions we make should be frequently interspersed with calls for His aid: "Holy Spirit, help me pray!" "Holy Spirit, help me understand what I am doing; I count on you for your grace right now."

If we are aware of conviction from the Holy Spirit over sins in our lives, we should certainly enter into confession and repentance over these. This is an appropriate preliminary to the further steps we take.

In seeking an enlargement of our fellowship with the Spirit of God, we must take a careful look at the reality of the flesh and its operation in our lives. Have we really faced up to the fact of rebellion and independency in our nature? Do we realize that this is an affliction which touches every part of our personalities? In our thinking processes we like to preserve our right to be independent; in our emotional reactions to people and situations we have that tendency. We have a push toward autonomy in our choices. We guard our right to private operation in the expression of our sexuality. We are not now talking about outward actions that are wrong. We are centering on the strong push of our sinful nature toward active godlessness. Knowing now that Christ entered into a positive dying to sin and independency, and that the Holy Spirit plans to bring into our lives the virtue and power of this dying, *are we willing that this be done?*

It is frequently true that there will be some particular area of our personal function that will show the deepest hold of the flesh on us. It often will be the place of greatest natural capacity. People with superior mental abilities will often find their greatest temptation to pride and independent self-confidence in their reasoning processes. Those with large emotional capacities will often find their personal battles strongest there. A person with a strong sex drive may find the idea of fellowship with God in this area of living most difficult to tolerate. Whatever the particular strong place may be in different persons, when a break comes there, it becomes much easier to go on to include the entire personality in this commitment.

In any case, by the Holy Spirit's help, and in the most total way possible, we must choose our place with Christ in His dying and make that response to God. A prayer toward this end might sound something like this: "Lord, by the help of the Holy Spirit, I choose my place in Jesus' dying to sin. I choose His death to all my rights to be independent. I take my place with Him at the cross, in death to my right to be independent in my thinking, in my feelings, in my choices, in my gratifying of bodily appetites. I choose that place; and, Spirit of God, I ask You to make Christ's dying real to me in all my life."

This is an overall, all-embracing stance. Jesus talked about taking up the cross *daily* in order to follow Him (Luke 9:23), and in some way we will need to set out each day with this choice of faith. One prayer of this sort, though indeed it may be climactic the first time it is uttered, does not guarantee the future of our walk with God. It does not eradicate the god-complex from our nature, but rather becomes a way of daily life.

As we are enabled, at some level, to make this over-all choice of conformity to Christ's death, we are then in a position to make a direct invitation to the Holy Spirit to be enthroned in all the functions of our being. Our prayer might sound like this: "Holy Spirit of God, I thank You for Your presence in my life. You have helped me now to take my place in Christ's death, and to renounce at Calvary my claim and desire for independency. So now I invite You to have fellowship with me in the whole function of my being, and in every part of it. Have fellowship with me in my thinking processes, in my feelings and choices. Have fellowship with me in the expression of my bodily appetites for food, sex, shelter, recreation, self-preservation, etc. I honor You as God in my life."

Let us remember at this point that what we are talking about is *fellowship*, not the wiping out of our personality. What *dies* is the god-right we have assumed. What *lives* is the basic person God created, set marvelously free in fellowship with God. To be sure, God is supreme; Christ is King; and we must be submitted to Him. Nevertheless we will be in a fellowship of whole persons.

Based on the instruction of James 4:7, having now submitted ourselves at the cross of God, we should turn and resist the devil, declaring ourselves free from his encroachments. This is not prayer to the devil; it is in no sense an entreaty. Rather, it is an exercise of the authority of Jesus Christ, to declare that the devil has no right to afflict our personality in any way. The kind of resistance called for in James 4:7 might sound like this: "Satan, in the name and authority of Jesus Christ, and by the help of the Holy Spirit, who in me is greater than you, I command you to relinquish any claim and any hold on my life. In Jesus' name, I declare myself free from you in my thinking, in my emotions, in my will, in the gratifying of my appetites—in my whole spirit, mind, and body. For this purpose was the Son of God manifested, to destroy your works, so I command you in Jesus' name to recognize your place of defeat in my life, you and all your agents." Don't make this any longer than necessary; don't plead with him; don't ask him. Take the authority of Jesus Christ and resist him by the Holy Spirit's help. He has no alternative, according to Scripture. "He will flee from you!"

There will be many crisis renewals of these responses that will become necessary. A good example is a situation in which you are seeking the Lord's direction in a decision. There may well be something in the matter that makes a strong appeal to your own desire, and which could easily push you over into the assertion of sovereignty in considering it. Very subtly indeed we can come to the point where we really want God's blessing on a plan of our own contriving, rather than to know what His plan is. To be sure that you are free to know His will and walk straight into it in fellowship with Him, it will be well to renew your stance at the cross regarding your independent rights, specifically in this decision, to honor the Holy Spirit's place in it, and to resist the deceiver. This will not relieve you of the need to look carefully at the data of the decision in fellowship with the Holy Spirit, nor of the need to pray until wisdom and clarity come into your thinking about it.

Another call for renewal arises when we are deeply hurt by some person or event. It is a most natural response to withdraw into independency when we are hurting. In effect we say, "Lord, look what happened to me! I have a right to feel the way I do. Now just leave me alone so that I can enjoy my misery (and my fantasies of revenge) by myself!" There is no doubt that we will have many hurts and sorrows in this life. But we have the unspeakable privilege of walking through them in fellowship with the Spirit of God. At such a moment, we need to turn deliberately to the Holy Spirit, take to the cross our independent desire, and invite Him to walk with us through the hurting time. Where He is, there is healing!

This is something of the direction in which we must go in seeking growth of our fellowship with God. By His Word He will show many refinements and deepenings of these responses. We will see areas of flesh of which we were not previously aware, but will know what to do about them. In the meantime, we will be knowing something of the glorious liberty of God's Spirit.

It is often helpful to have a fellow-Christian praying with us and encouraging us in the processes described above. This need not be a professional or pastoral counselor, so long as there is mutual understanding of what is being done. The helper-Christian can often give us the word of encouragement or wisdom at points where we are about to get bogged down and help us stay on track. There is also power in joint prayers and comfort in sensing together the relief that the Holy Spirit gives.

The question of what to do in response to these truths *on the community level* is one which needs much attention in our day. The writer feels deeply this need himself, as though we stand at the edge of an unexplored ocean of grace and have only glimpses of its size.

The fact that there is a community dimension of knowing God suggests that we ought to be giving serious attention to the way community attention to the Word and to prayer will build that experience. What it means to be "speaking to one another in psalms and hymns and spiritual songs" at the same time that we are "singing and making melody in our hearts to the Lord" (Eph. 5:19, NASB), challenges our understanding of corporate worship. The delicate balance by which authority structures in the Christian community are to function in the full exercise of spiritual dynamics is one in which we have much need to grow. Many a board of spiritual overseers in a local church needs to face up to the fact that they *in their board functions do not interact as a community of Christians.* Here is probably the place where the display of Christian community is most important and hardest to come by in the local church!

Just what it means to go on collective ego trips is worth some serious study. Here we need to understand what repentance and confession mean on the community level—indeed what it means to share Christ's dying, not only as individuals, but as groups.

In the meantime, while we move toward a greater understanding of these matters, we can surely seek to be those who channel into the Christian community the healing stream of Christ's love, His attitudes of acceptance, forgiveness, longsuffering, and joy. We can seek to affirm one another's gifts and ministries, to recognize and delight in the presence of Christ in each other.

Also we can seek those less known characteristics of mutual admonition, productive discipline, and the "binding and loosing" type of prayer. Our churches must become places where the Spirit of God is known and loved, for this He deeply wants.

"He has showed you, O man, what is good. And what does the Lord require of you? To act justly and to love mercy and to walk humbly with your God" (Micah 6:8, NIV). To act justly and to love mercy, we expect God to require of us. But for Him to require us to walk in fellowship with Him astounds us. He *wants* this! He wants to be known and loved! He wants interaction with us.

Looking at our human miseries we become pessimistic that this can ever occur in this life. The kind of nature we have; the active opposition of a superior being, Satan; the hemming in of an evil and ungodly world—these are enough to make us shake our heads in gloom.

But Scripture changes all that by showing us a Savior who has triumphed gloriously over all our foes, who is alive in great glory and beauty. It shows us the beautiful reality of the union that exists between us and Him— the very presence of His Spirit in our lives. The Savior touches us with His glory even now as we believe in Him. The possibilities are not to be measured in terms of our weakness, or even the strength of the enemy and the world, but in terms of Jesus' victory, power, and glory. These are strong grounds—the very strongest

indeed—for hope and for expectation of genuine
fellowship with our God, here and now.
Let us take hold of this with joy.
May the glory of our Lord
Jesus Christ shine
in your
life!